Books should be returned on or before the
last date stamped below

06 AUG 02

02 AUG 03

09. OCT 03.

−4 DEC 2003

−8 JUL 2004

−3 AUG 2004
27 JAN 2005
−3 MAY 2005
26 JUL 2005
18 MAY 2006
12 JUN 2006
24 AUG 2006
−2 DEC 2006

15 MAY 2007
19 JUN 2007
16 JUL 2007
22 SEP 2007
12 JAN 2008
17 MAY 2008
−1 SEP 2008
−8 NOV 2008
25 NOV 2008
12 JAN 2009
−2 MAR 2009
21 MAR 2009

ABERDEENSHIRE LIBRARY
AND INFORMATION SERVICE
MELDRUM MEG WAY, OLDMELDRUM

Foley, Caroline

Practical
allotment
gardening : a
                635.
                0484
1278105

D0548591

Practical
# ALLOTMENT
Gardening

# Practical
# ALLOTMENT
# Gardening

**A guide to growing fruit, vegetables and herbs on your plot**

# CAROLINE FOLEY

SPECIAL PHOTOGRAPHY BY CLIVE NICHOLS

**New Holland**

*To allotment holders everywhere*

*and to my daughters,*

*Catherine and Francesca*

First published in 2002 by
New Holland Publishers (UK) Ltd
London · Cape Town · Sydney · Auckland

Garfield House
86–88 Edgware Road
London W2 2EA
United Kingdom

80 McKenzie Street
Cape Town 8001
South Africa

Level 1, Unit 4, 14 Aquatic Drive
Frenchs Forest, NSW 2086
Australia

218 Lake Road
Northcote, Auckland
New Zealand

Text copyright © 2002 Caroline Foley
Copyright © 2002 New Holland Publishers (UK) Ltd

The right of Caroline Foley to be identified as the
author of this work has been asserted by her in
accordance with the Copyright, Designs and
Patents Act, 1988

All rights reserved. No part of this publication
may be reproduced, stored in a retrieval system,
or transmitted in any form or by any means,
electronic, mechanical, photocopying, recording
or otherwise, without the prior written permission
of the publishers and copyright holders.

ISBN 1 85974 890 2

Editor: Sandra Raphael
Designer: Lisa Tai
Special photographer: Clive Nichols
Picture researcher: Joanne Beardwell
Illustrations: Kate Simunek

Editorial Direction: Rosemary Wilkinson
Project Editor: Clare Johnson
Production: Hazel Kirkman

10 9 8 7 6 5 4 3 2 1

Reproduction by Modern Age Repro, Hong Kong
Printed and bound by Times Offset (M) Sdn Bhd,
Malaysia

*half title page:* A scarecrow keeps birds away on this allotment.

*title page:* Neat rows of vegetables in well-tended plots are visible on this allotment site, viewed from above.

*above:* Allotment owners are often very resourceful: here recycled plastic bottles are turned into effective bird-scarers.

635.0484
1278105

## Photography credits

**Caroline Foley:** 5, 9, 10, 13t, 15t, 19b, 24tr & b, 51tr, 63b, 67t; **Flowers & Foliage:** 44t, 51tl; **Garden Picture Library:** L Burgess 91b; D Cavagnaro 21; J Glover 87; M Howes 1; J Hurst 11, 34t; H Rice 70/front cover; A Scaresbrook 12b; J Wade 18b/back cover; P Windsor 65; **John Glover:** 15br, 27t, 35, 55tl, 69b, 74, 92; **Holt Studios:** R Anthony 42b, 54; A Burridge 72; N Cattlin 24tl, 30t, 40b, 41t, 42t, 47, 77t & c, 82, 84, 85; B Gibbons 49t, 75; W Harinck 31b; M Mayer 89b; R Mayer 20, 58, 73t; **David Markson:** 50t, 93 (Yalding Organic Gardens, Kent); **Peter McHoy:** 14, 80; **Clive Nichols:** 6, 8, 15bl, 18t (Yalding Organic Gardens, Kent), 19t, 25t (Yalding), 26, 27b (Yalding), 28-29, 30b (Yalding), 32-33, 37l (Yalding), 37r, 39/front cover, 40t (Yalding), 41b, 43t, 44b/back cover, 45t, 46b, 48/back cover, 51b/front cover, 52, 55tr, 55b (Yalding), 56bl & br, 59 (Yalding), 66, 68 (Yalding), 71b, 76 (Yalding), 77b (Yalding), 78t, 79b (Yalding), 81, 91t; **Photos Horticultural:** 22, 23t, 24tc, 25b, 31t & c, 38, 46t, 49bl, 56t, 60, 63t, 73b, 89t, 90; **Sea Spring Photos:** 34b, 43b, 53/front cover, 61, 62, 64, 88; **Harry Smith:** 2-3, 12t, 23b, 57, 67b, 71t; **Derek St Romaine:** 13b, 16, 36t/front cover, 36b (Hampton Court Flower Show 1998, Leyhill Prison), 45b, 49br, 50b.

# CONTENTS

# INTRODUCTION

One bright July morning I found myself sitting on an upturned log on a London allotment site. The sun was warm on my face and bees and butterflies were about. I could have reached out and picked a raspberry or a blackcurrant. The only sound was the chorus of birds. Having just escaped the noise of rush-hour traffic in the steamy streets outside, I felt I was in the Garden of Eden.

Around me were rows of vegetables, potatoes in flower, cabbages and kale – the very heart of allotment gardening. Some plots reflected individual interests. A dahlia fanatic grew blooms the size of dinner-plates, a doctor cultivated sweet peas for his surgery, and a young mother grew flowers to decorate her church and to make dried arrangements to sell at a school fête. Dotted around were ornamental lettuces, crossed poles of runner beans in fiery flower and the dramatic heads of globe artichokes. Sweet peppers were ripening under old window-frames alongside aubergines and melons.

Allotments are oases in the city and an antidote to stress. They offer a satisfying occupation for the retired, soil and sunshine for people who live in high-rise flats, a lifeline for those stuck in offices all week – and friendship. Gardening is an interest which crosses all barriers.

We must be careful not to lose our allotments. Those on prime city sites offer rich pickings for developers. In England, statutory allotment sites seem to be safe as a decision to close one can be

△ Allotments are oases in the city, places to unwind and grow produce that is fresher, healthier, cheaper and much more delicious than you can buy.

made only by the Secretary of State. It's the temporary sites that are most at risk.

All too often they slip through the net when the threatened plot-holders fail to galvanize themselves in time or alert allies to their cause. Sometimes sites slide into dereliction, left open to vandalism and theft. If there is no water supply, there may be a lack of willing customers. If there is no apparent demand, it is difficult to make a case. Yet when people put up a fight, miracles can happen. The most famous reprieve was that of New York's Guerilla Gardens when film actress Bette Midler swept in at the eleventh hour, cheque book in hand.

Allotments have a long tradition, springing from the need to provide a small piece of land for the labouring poor to grow food. In England they started erratically in the 18th century when the Enclosure Acts took away the right of villagers to common land. By the mid-19th century they had become established throughout Europe. With industrialization, they sprang up around many towns. In the First and Second World Wars every scrap of land, from park to private garden, became an allotment. Dig for Victory campaigns were widespread across Europe and America.

In the 21st century the emphasis is changing. Whereas allotments still play a vital role in feeding the poor across the world, in mainland Europe many have become leisure gardens, with chalets surrounded by ornamental plants. Overall, they are less to do with survival and more about how we choose to live, with the benefits to health of fresh air and exercise and the desire to provide our families with fresh food.

The case for organic gardening is clear. It is becoming a tidal wave. Food scares, often caused by intensive farming methods, have shaken complacency and resulted in a distrust of what may end up on our plates. One way out of it is to buy organic produce. An even better way is to grow your own – it's fresher and cheaper.

Concerns for wildlife, and the environmental legacy we leave for future generations, have made people reconsider lifelong habits. Buying food that's flown in from the other side of the world is a waste of resources, as is the staggering amount of household rubbish that goes into landfill sites. Most of that could be composted for the benefit of our plants instead of giving rise to harmful greenhouse gases.

Organic gardening is about working with nature. Instead of killing off the good bugs with the bad and damaging the environment, the idea is to attract useful predators to work for you. Building up a soil vibrant with microscopic life, by adding masses of compost, will make the plants flourish without chemical fertilizers, and the worms will do the digging. As organic gardening is as old as the hills, there may seem to be nothing new to learn. With its revival, however, helpful new ideas and techniques have sprung up.

I see an allotment as a cross between a domestic garden and a smallholding and techniques from both disciplines are useful. An allotment is large enough to borrow practices from agriculture yet small enough for plants to be tended individually. Traditionally, allotment holders have regarded it as a matter of pride to be self-sufficient. In that spirit, I have tried to find the cheapest ways to do things, but when it seems better to buy I have said so.

Keeping up a plot can be physically demanding, but the rewards are tangible. There is nothing quite so delicious as fruit and vegetables picked at their peak and eaten when young, or cooked straight away. You cannot buy them that fresh. Once their sugar has turned to starch, much of the flavour is lost. Fruit ripened in the sun, rather than the warehouse, is out of this world, beyond comparison with most on sale. Allotmenteers dine like royalty and have perhaps the greatest satisfaction of all. They can truly enjoy the fruits of their labour.

Taking on a new allotment can be quite a challenge, particularly if it has been neglected. It's all too easy to lose heart trying to tackle the whole thing in one go, so make a plan of priorities and work through them in your own time.

# the new plot

◁ Sweet peas and chrysanthemums are popular choices for those who enjoy flowers as well as fresh produce for the table.

# ASSESSING the site

**Before you make a start on planting, plan carefully where to put the main components: the greenhouse, the shed, compost bins, vegetable beds and the paths. It will save time and effort in the long run.**

> • INITIAL PLANNING
>
> • PATHS  Mown grass, Trampled earth, Paving slabs
>
> • SITE CHECKLIST
>
> • **PROJECT ~ *Edging boards***
>
> • WATER
>
> • **PROJECT ~ *Making a pond***
>
> • COMPOST AND MANURE HEAPS

## INITIAL PLANNING

Before taking on a new plot, find out if there is a choice of allotment sites in your area and visit them all. They do vary. Some are in beautiful places with a view, but they may be exposed to howling winds; others are tucked down alley-ways, surrounded by houses but with the advantage of shelter. Many run along railway lines or are on old bomb-sites. They are to be found in all sorts of unexpected places.

The facilities on offer vary from a smart club-house down to nothing at all. Some sites have a trading shed where various supplies are provided at wholesale prices. A well run allotment commit-tee might bring in manure, wood shavings in bulk, supplies of pallets and even old carpets.

There may be high fences and secure locks to keep out vandals, communal compost heaps, seed-sharing schemes and a wildlife area. Some committees have equipment to lend, put on entertainment or produce a newsletter.

Once you've procured your plot, think about how you will use it. Take into consideration the amount of time you will spend there. Be realistic. If you can get there only at weekends, there is no point in planting produce that needs daily atten-tion in summer unless you can persuade someone to share the work with you. Would you like to grow flowers for the house? Will you be spending time there in summer evenings? If so, a plot with a sheltered west-facing corner to catch the evening sun would be ideal.

△ Once the expensive structures such as greenhouse and shed have been placed, work out where the beds and paths should go, arranging them to make most efficient use of space while maintaining easy access to all parts of the allotment.

In the beginning, gather all the information that you can about the site. Allotments come in various sizes and are usually rectangular strips. Draw the plot out roughly to scale and make photocopies or tracings of the diagram. The first plan will show the ground as it is. Get your bearings and mark them in with a sign pointing north. Is the plot exposed? Check the regional climate and the direction of the prevailing winds. Walk around the site and mark in weed-infested areas, boggy bits or anything else of note. Find out what you can from the neighbours. Mark all that you have gleaned on the plan. On the second plan work out where you want to put the permanent features – the shed, paths, the main beds and so on. Reserve a third copy of the plan for plants.

## PATHS

The main paths should take the most direct routes from greenhouse to shed to compost heap, and from the water-butt to the flower and vegetable beds, with plenty of room to get a wheelbarrow past. Narrower paths are fine between beds or to clip a hedge without treading on the soil. You do see the occasional plot with

### SITE CHECKLIST
- Check whether the future of the allotment site is secure.
- Look at the rules. They vary from country to country, town to town and site to site.  A common decree forbids trees in case they can shade other plots.
- Is the allotment organic? If not, will you be right next to someone who sprays everything in sight?
- What is the situation with sheds and greenhouses? Perhaps you could take over a greenhouse from a previous occupant.
- Are the neighbouring plots covered in weeds which will scatter seed all over yours?
- What are the watering facilities?
- Are there restrictions on what you may grow?
- Are you expected to put in some hours for odd jobs?
- Can you start with half a plot?

▽ Plan the main path to follow the most convenient routes with room to get past with a wheelbarrow.

permanent paths of brick or paving, but it would be much more sensible to start off with the cheaper option of temporary paths which can be moved if you change your mind about where you want to put them.

• **Mown grass** makes attractive paths but needs constant mowing and edging.

• **Trampled earth** is fine for less important paths, along a fruit hedge for example, and you can change your mind about them at will. If you have problems with weeds or soggy soil, you can make a temporary cover for these areas with straw or newspapers weighed down with grass cuttings or wood shavings.

• **Old paving slabs** can be laid straight on the ground on a bed of sand. You don't need to cement them in until you are sure that you know where you want them.

▷ Narrow raised beds, made from logs, are separated by access paths and allow the gardener to reach all parts of the beds without treading on the soil and thus compacting it. Wood chippings over a weed-suppressing cover form paths that are pleasant to walk on and will not need to be weeded.

◁ Old carpet kills even the worst weeds by depriving them of light and makes a temporary path that is firm and comfortable to use. It will, however, eventually rot.

◁ Old paving slabs make solid paths which will last a long time. If they are simply laid on earth, without mortar filling the gaps between them, however, weeds may be a problem.

# • PROJECT •
## EDGING BOARDS

Edging boards are a good way to divide the paths from the beds and are easy to make. Use old floorboards, railway sleepers, logs or timber offcuts. They will keep soil off the paths and path material off the beds. A low edging will divide paths from beds but if you make it higher you will produce raised beds. The advantage of these is that you can concentrate on improving the soil in a localized way where it is most needed for a particular crop. If the beds are narrow enough to reach across, you won't need to tread on them and damage the soil by compacting it.

### You will need
- edging boards
- short posts
- weed-suppressant matting
- loose surfacing material
- topsoil and compost

**1** Mark out the areas that you want to use as beds.

**2** Drive the posts well into the ground and nail the edging boards onto the outside so that the posts don't form a hazard.

**3** Lay a cover on the paths to suppress weeds. Horticultural membrane, heavy-duty black polythene or face-down hessian-backed carpet will do the trick.

**4** Cover the path area with a loose surface material such as gravel, chipped bark, wood shavings or sawdust.

**5** Fill the beds with good topsoil and compost.

## WATER

Rainwater is the best for plants. Saving it is a good policy, not only for water conservation, but for practical reasons. In many allotments there are only scattered tanks or standpipes, which means watering by hand. In summer, when everybody wants to water plants at the same time, there can be real shortages and mounting frustration as queues form.

Plan for as many barrels as you can fit in to catch water. If you have a shed or a greenhouse put in a down pipe to channel the water from the guttering of the roof. A tap on the water-butt makes life easier though you may need to raise

# • PROJECT •
## MAKING A POND

A small pond will help to create a balanced environment by bringing in birds and other useful creatures to the allotment. A few frogs or toads, for example, will help to deal effectively with a slug problem. Site the pond in a sunny area, away from trees to prevent leaves dropping into it. In cold countries make it at least 60 cm (2 ft) deep at some point to prevent the whole pond freezing in winter.

An old stone sink, a galvanized cattle trough or any large container sunk into the ground will make a pond. Another option is to buy a flexible butyl liner.

When the pond is finished, put in a plank or make shelves with stones and large pebbles to allow creatures to get in an out. Add frog spawn, but no fish as they will eat the tadpoles. Native plants, both in the pond and around the margins, are a good addition for wildlife. Cover the pond with heavy-duty mesh wire to make it safe for children.

### You will need

- a flexible butyl liner
- spade for digging
- sand or an old carpet
- heavy stones for edging
- planks or large pebbles
- pond plants
- frog spawn

**1** Dig a hole for the flexible liner, remove sharp stones and sticks and anything else that might pierce the liner. Remember to make a shallow place in the pond for birds and other creatures to bathe and drink.

**2** Cover the excavation with a layer of sand or old carpet as extra protection and lay on the liner, moulding it into the right shape.

**3** Throw a little subsoil in the bottom and fill the pond with water. Try to get a bucketful from an established pond to speed up the development of the new pond's ecology.

**4** When the pond is full, secure and disguise the liner round the edges with heavy stones, filling in gaps with soil.

◁ A downpipe from the roof of the shed into a water butt is useful for providing your own water supply, but it should be disconnected in winter to prevent flooding.

the barrel on bricks or some other base to get a watering can underneath the tap. To avoid flooding, put an overflow pipe near the rim of the butt to divert the water into a second container or to a channel to water the plants. Cover the barrels to prevent them getting choked with fallen leaves.

## COMPOST AND MANURE HEAPS

Compost is the great soil enhancer. Allow space for two or three generous compost bins in an accessible place near a wide path so that you can get to them easily with a wheelbarrow. If the site is sloping, put the heaps on the lower level as compost is lighter to move when it has rotted down. Compost heaps can be a bit smelly, and so can a manure heap, so put them as far away as possible from the sitting area.

Manure is usually delivered by road, so the ideal place for a heap of it is the nearest point to the road where it can be tipped.

◁ △ Site the compost bin and the manure heap as far as possible from the sitting area. If your site is on a slope, put them at the bottom as the contents become lighter as they rot down.

# PLANNING
# the beds

**Different plants have different needs. Annual vegetables and flowers need good soil and plenty of sun; soft fruit and herbaceous perennials are less fussy, while salad leaves like some shade.**

- ANNUAL VEGETABLE BEDS

- THE PERFECT PLOT

- PERMANENT FEATURES
  Asparagus
  Fruit trees
  Seed beds
  Soft fruit
  Strawberries

- PERENNIALS AND HERB BEDS

Once you have worked out where to put the more permanent features on the allotment and decided what the most convenient routes between them are, the next step is to put the main types of plants into groups according to their needs.

## ANNUAL VEGETABLE BEDS

First choose the site for annual vegetables. They do a marathon in a single season and need five-star conditions, the best and sunniest south-facing area that you can provide. You need four, or even better five, beds for a rotation scheme (see chapter 3, p. 35). The beds should face north/south so that the plants don't shade each other and get the maximum amount of sun.

Soft fruit and herbaceous perennials can go around them.

The idea is to divide the plants into their botanical family groups. As they are related, each group is likely to be attacked by the same pests and diseases. By moving them around you can minimize the chances of a soil infestation. Alternating plants with deep tap roots, such as carrots and parsnips, with those with shallow fibrous roots is good for soil structure. As these plants are annuals, you will be able to clear the beds and start afresh each year, and over time you will discover which are the best crops for your conditions.

Raised beds are particularly good for plants in a rotation scheme. The soil will be rich and deep, encouraging the roots to grow downwards. In

△ Cosmos and pot marigolds growing among spinach, sweetcorn and red cabbages in cottage garden style. If the soil is kept healthy and fertile, you will be able to pack in the plants

## THE PERFECT PLOT

In this plan you enter from the bottom end where there is a manure heap, compost bins, a wildlife area, comfrey, an extra water-butt and some soft fruit. A path that is wide enough for a barrow runs up to the top of the plot, past the rotation beds. These run from north to south for maximum sun and so that the plants don't shade each other. Then you come to the more ornamental area where taller plants give some screening. Behind them, and facing west for the evening sun, there is a seat backed by the non-prickly cane fruits and a small pond. This is the utility area with the greenhouse, the cold frame and seed bed, which need to face south, and the shed and water-butts.

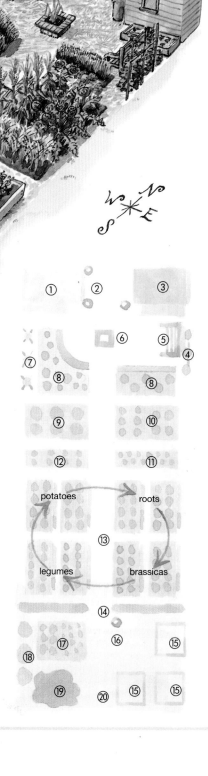

## PLANTING THE ALLOTMENT

① greenhouse
② water-butts with downpipes from roof
③ shed with seed bed in front
④ cane fruits
⑤ bench facing west for evening sun
⑥ pond in sunny area
⑦ cane fruits
⑧ flowers and ornamental vegetable bed with lavender hedge for scent and bees
⑨ bush fruit
⑩ sweetcorn and globe artichokes – tall plants to provide some privacy
⑪ asparagus
⑫ strawberries
⑬ vegetable on rotation – potatoes, legumes, brassicas and roots on raised beds narrow enough to reach across with room to get round the back, facing N/S
⑭ low hedge made from prunings and covered with ivy for wildlife
⑮ compost
⑯ additional water-butt
⑰ comfrey bed and wild flowers
⑱ soft fruits
⑲ manure heap
⑳ wide central path with room for a wheelbarrow

△ Lettuces grow fast and don't like to be in hot sun. You can grow them in their own bed as shown here or intercrop them between slower-growing vegetables.

this way you can get more into the space and the leaf cover will help to smother the weeds.

Cut flowers, if they are hardy annuals, will need prime conditions of plenty of sun, good drainage and rich soil.

## PERMANENT FEATURES

• **Asparagus** is a perennial crop, and once established an asparagus bed will continue to produce delicious spears for about twenty years.

Choose a sunny site with good drainage.

• **Fruit trees** If the allotment rules allow it and you have room, a small fruit tree will add variety to the plot and will also be of benefit to wildlife, or you might like to train fruit trees as cordons to make a division (see chapter 4, p. 59).

• **Seed beds** are very useful for bringing on young plants before they go into their permanent positions. Put it in a sheltered sunny spot, near the greenhouse if you have one. Fit the cold frame into the same kind of situation.

• **Soft fruit** With the exception of strawberries, soft fruit grows on bushes, canes or briars. The cane fruits (red-, white- and blackcurrants and raspberries) and the briar fruits (blackberries, loganberries and other hybrids) need support. You could make a fruit fence for privacy or to divide the plot into different areas. Soft fruit needs to be protected from birds with netting; if you want to grow a lot you might want to construct a fruit cage. Soft fruit will tolerate a little shade, but not frost pockets.

• **Strawberries** should be moved every three years and they like an airy, sunny spot.

▷ A good mixture of flowers and herbs among the vegetables makes the allotment plot both ecologically friendly and prettier. Flowers will attract pollinating insects and friendly predators, such as hoverflies, ladybirds and lacewings, all of which eat aphids and other pests.

## PERENNIALS AND HERB BEDS

Use the remaining space for more permanent perennials, flowers and herbs. If you have planned a seating area, you will probably want to have the prettiest and most highly scented plants around it. If there is room, find a little corner for a few comfrey plants – they make a wonderful free fertilizer if they are dug in later.

Salads don't like to be roasted in the sun. Slot them in (as an intercrop) between slow-growing crops where they will enjoy a little shade from the leaves of taller plants.

Wildlife is the best friend of the organic gardener so keep it in mind from the start, if only to help in dealing with pests. Provide some undisturbed corners: a few logs in a corner will make a home for many insects, as will the odd stone left

△ A well-stocked plot in late summer with Swiss chard and runner beans on poles in full production.

▷ In Holland you sometimes see wildlife habitats made out of old twiggy prunings, piled up between stakes.

unturned or a hedge or some shrubs for cover. In Holland they make elegant low hedges out of their prunings, piling twigs and branches between pegs and growing ivy over it. A little verge of uncut grass will make a refuge for spiders, beetles and other insects. Thick mulches will encourage centipedes and beetles to make homes. They eat slugs and will do a good job on both larvae and eggs. Make nests for aphid-eating hoverflies and parasitic wasps out of bunches of hollow sticks tied together.

The secret of organic gardening lies in the soil. Good soil is teeming with micro-organisms, as well as vegetable and animal remains, air and water. The key to achieving high fertility is to feed the soil and let it feed the plants.

# the soil

2

## ALL YOU NEED TO KNOW ABOUT SOIL
Soil types
Topsoil
Acid or alkaline?

## WEEDS
Perennial weeds
Annual weeds
Clearing grass
**PROJECT –** *How and when to dig*

## HUMUS, MUCK AND MULCHING
Compost
**PROJECT –** *Making a compost heap*
Compost contents
Mulches
Types of manure
Green manures

◁ Allotments in countries with warmer climates, such as this one in Madeira, need constant irrigation to be productive.

# ALL YOU NEED TO KNOW
## about soil

**This section shows you how to find out about your soil with a few simple tests. The key points to know are its structure, how deep the topsoil is and whether it is acid or alkaline. Once you know its character, it is easy to improve it if you need to.**

- SOIL TYPES
  Chalk
  Clay soil
  Loam
  Peat
  Sandy soil
  Silt

- TOPSOIL

- ACID OR ALKALINE?

## SOIL TYPES

On taking over a site, find out as much as you can about the soil. A good crop of weeds, especially nettles, is an indication of fertility. Dig up a few spadefuls to check on the worms. If they are plentiful and a healthy pink, you are off to a good start. You can learn quite a bit about the soil by picking up a small handful half an hour after it has rained and squeezing it. Try to roll it into a sausage and make a ring.

- **Chalk** won't keep the shape of its mould and is usually full of flintstones. It is very free-draining and limey which makes it alkaline and inhospitable to many plants. It's poor soil. Add lots of humus and consider raised beds.

- **Clay soil** will feel sticky and will keep the shape of its mould. It is rich in minerals and holds on to nutrients and water. It doesn't drain well, it is slow to warm up after winter and it cakes in the heat. Raised beds that you can reach across will help because treading on this kind of soil will make things worse. Digging it over in the autumn and letting the winter weather do its worst will break it down. The addition of sharp sand or grit and lots of organic matter will help with drainage and texture.

- **Loam** is the ideal. A lump of it will take an imprint from your hand and break into crumbs. It is dark brown – a good mixture of sand (for drainage) and clay (for nutrients and moisture).

- **Peat** is dark and spongy and doesn't keep the shape of its mould. Full of organic matter, it is

△ By continually adding compost to any type of soil, the beds will eventually become raised and the soil will become rich and friable, giving both ornamentals and edibles the best possible conditions.

fertile though low in minerals. Easy to work, it dries out quickly and is acid. Adding lime will make it more alkaline.

• **Sandy soil** is gritty to the touch and won't stay in the shape of a roll. Free-draining and easy to work, it warms up quickly in spring. Adding humus will help to bind the particles together and retain nutrients and moisture. If you need to dig, leave it till spring to prevent the soil being leached by rainwater.

• **Silt** feels silky. It will make a ring of sorts and should be treated like clay.

## TOPSOIL

Dig a hole to check the depth of the topsoil, the layer that feeds the plants. Beneath it is the sub-soil which is lighter in colour and contains few nutrients, though its structure affects drainage. If you think that there is not enough topsoil, raise the beds. An ideal depth is 60 cm (2 ft).

△ Soil should be friable so that plants and worms can push their way through easily. If the soil is compacted and airless, either make raised beds or break it down by hand.

△ Pick up a handful of moist soil and study the texture to find out what type of soil you have.

### ACID OR ALKALINE?

Test the pH to find out whether the soil is acid or alkaline. The best reading for most plants is 5.5 to 7.5. A pH of 7 is neutral; above 7 is alkaline and below 7 is acid. Potatoes, broad beans and peppers prosper in slightly acid soil whereas celery and cauliflower prefer alkaline. While you can tip the balance and improve the soil, you cannot completely change its character. However, you can choose plants which prefer your particular type.

1 Collect three or four samples of soil from different parts of the plot. You can send them off for a full analysis but a cheap kit from a gardening centre is probably all you need.

2 If the soil is too acid, add lime; the quantity needed depends on both the type of soil and the acid level. Ground limestone (dolomitic lime) or calcified seaweed, which has trace elements in it, are expensive but they last a few years in the soil. Slaked lime (garden lime) or hydrated lime (builder's lime) need to be replaced annually. Do not add lime at the same time as manure as this prompts a harmful reaction between the two materials.

3 If the soil is too alkaline, garden manure and compost will send it in the right direction.

△ Ground elder

△ Couch grass

△ Horsetail

# WEEDS

Check your weeds as some are simple to remove, but others will plague you unless you take firm action straight away. If you don't have time to weed, at least remove flowers to prevent seeding.

- PERENNIAL WEEDS
- ANNUAL WEEDS
- CLEARING GRASS
- **PROJECT ~ *How and when to dig***

▽ When clearing grass, stack the turves upside down in a neat heap. They will soon rot down to form valuable loam.

## PERENNIAL WEEDS

- **Bindweed** *(Convolvulus arvensis)* is popular with bees, but it will twine around and strangle your plants in no time. If you follow it you will find an extensive tangle of creeping white roots.
- **Couch grass** *(Elymus repens)* spreads by underground rhizomes so tough that they can grow through a potato.
- **Creeping thistle** *(Circium arvense)* might look innocent, but its tap root sends out new shoots and it can spread at an alarming rate.
- **Docks** *(Rumex obtusifolius)* quickly grow a giant tap root and can produce 60,000 seeds a year.
- **Ground elder** *(Aegopodium podagraria)* travels in much the same way, as does **horsetail** *(Equisetum)* which likes damp ground.

Don't rotavate the ground because that will chop up the roots and spread the problem. Either deprive perennial weeds of light for a season (sometimes longer) by covering them with old carpet or heavy black plastic, or dig the plants out carefully with all their roots.

## ANNUAL WEEDS

Keep these in check with hoeing, hand-weeding and mulching. Warm a patch that you are planning to plant early by covering it with black polythene and watering the soil; you will encourage weed seeds to germinate. You can then pull up the weeds before planting.

## CLEARING GRASS

If you need to remove grass, take off the turf and bury it upside down about a spit (that is, the depth of a spade) below the surface and cover it with topsoil. It will rot down into lovely loam. You can also make loam by stacking turves upside down in a heap. Another method to kill off the grass is by covering it with black plastic, carpet, flattened cardboard boxes or newspaper weighed down with grass mowings, and wait a season before cultivating the area.

◁ Greedy feeders such as potatoes, courgettes and pumpkins can be planted in holes made in a turf stack. They will grow happily while the stack rots down into loam which can be returned to the soil.

# • PROJECT •

## HOW AND WHEN TO DIG

Too much digging can break your back and harm the soil structure. Follow these tips to decide how and when to dig:
• If the land is in good condition and free of pernicious weeds, don't dig at all.
• If the soil has been neglected and drainage is poor, consider double-digging just once to completely remove the weeds and to break up the subsoil.
• If the soil is in reasonable condition, single dig once, then follow the no-digging method.

### You will need

- a spade
- a fork
- a wheelbarrow
- compost or manure
- pegs and string

### Double digging

**1** Mark out a workable strip. Taking a small section at a time, dig up one spit (a spade's depth) of topsoil, remove any weed roots, and take the soil to the far end of the strip in a barrow.

**2** Break up the newly revealed subsoil with a fork.

**3** Moving on to the next section, dig up the top soil, remove any weed roots and put the soil in the first trench with some compost or manure.

**4** Proceed down the whole length of the patch, finally tipping the topsoil in the barrow into the last trench. Avoid mixing topsoil with the subsoil.

### Single digging

**1** Break up and turn the soil over one spit deep, removing weeds with their roots.

**2** Add rotted manure or compost as you go.

### No digging

Once the soil is workable you can relax and get the worms to do your digging.

**1** Put a good layer of rotted compost on the beds in autumn. The worms will take it down into the soil, making vertical channels for air and water to get to plant roots.

**2** Rake it over in the spring. Alternatively, use the compost as a weed- suppressing mulch through the growing season. Gradually, the beds will become raised.

# HUMUS, MUCK and mulching

In nature, compost is made slowly as plants and creatures die, eggs drop out of nests, leaves fall and birds leave their droppings. As everything rots down, a rich cycle of micro-life builds up making the soil fertile.

- COMPOST
- **PROJECT ~ *Making a compost heap***
- COMPOST CONTENTS
- MULCHES
- TYPES OF MANURE
- GREEN MANURES

The effect of adding humus in the form of well rotted compost and manure to the soil is a cumulative one. You will not only see great benefits in the first season, but you will also see ever greater ones in the years to come.

## COMPOST

Compost is satisfying to make. The vital ingredients are air circulation, moisture (there is usually enough in the green material but you might need to add water in dry periods), bacteria (there should be enough on the small amount of soil that clings to the roots of weeds that you put into the heap) and heat. A compost heap decomposes much faster in summer. Cover it to keep the heat in with a lid, plastic sheeting (or 'duvets' of plastic sacks stuffed with straw or balls of newspaper), or a piece of carpet. A sprinkling of lime every few layers will keep it sweet. Though an activator in the form of nitrogen is not strictly essential, it will speed things up. A layer of rotted compost from an old heap is excellent. Poultry manure and human urine work like magic. Nettles, seaweed meal, and blood, fish and bone meal are good too.

- **Compost bins** Make two, or even three compost bins for compost in different stages – one ready, one rotting down and one in the making. You can make compost on open ground but a container keeps it tidy, and the heap will need less turning as the edges won't dry out. You need a container without a bottom (so the worms can

△ A simple but practical compost bin is made out of interlocking planks of recycled wood with notches cut into them to hold them together. This compost bin is easy to dismantle, making it simple to remove the compost.

# • PROJECT •

## MAKING A COMPOST HEAP

If there is a communal compost heap it might be possible to fill it all in one day, the most effective method. Making good compost is simply a question of gauging how much of each ingredient to put in and keeping an eye on it while it 'cooks'.

### You will need

- two or three compost bins
- straw or twiggy weeds
- green material such as grass clippings
- lime
- compost activator

**1** Aim for layers of different materials. Start the heap with something coarse – straw or twiggy weeds to let in air. Never add too much of one thing at a time. If you put in a layer of grass cuttings, which may go soggy, mix it with torn and wetted newspaper or soaked straw. Sprinkle on lime or activator every few layers.

**2** Watch the heap. See that it doesn't get too dry or too wet. If it smells, it's probably too wet, so turn it over to let some air in and add straw or newspaper. If it's too dry, pour on some water or add fresh green material or grass cuttings. Don't let it turn into an airless solid block!

**3** If you're not happy with the mixture, tip it all out onto a large plastic sheet, mix it well, add whatever it seems to need and put it back. Turn from sides to middle, middle to sides about two weeks later. You'll know when it's ready. It won't smell, it will be dark brown, crumbly and pleasant to handle – nectar for plants. You won't recognize the ingredients and there will be plenty of little red worms having a field day.

get in), air circulation, a lid or cover, and access from the side or top to turn the compost and get it out. Allotment holders are resourceful and usually manage to get hold of useful material – by hook or crook – floorboards, old pallets and things like that.

A simple bin can be made by tying pallets together at the corners and stuffing straw or cardboard down the gaps. A more sophisticated version is the New Zealand box. Nail together three pallets into a cube and bang in two posts in the front. Slide boards between the posts and the pallets to make a 'door'. You can make a less attractive but functional compost bin out of old tyres. Cut off the walls or sides of the tyres, then turn them inside out and stack them up.

◁ A compost bin made from a strip of wire sheep netting tied round with carpet. This allows air to reach the compost as it rots, and is cheap and easy to make at home. The top should be covered with another piece of carpet to retain the heat.

## COMPOST CONTENTS

Almost anything organic from the household can be added to a compost heap – kitchen scraps, tea, coffee, eggshells, wood ash, hair, paper and cardboard, natural fabrics (torn up and soaked), all soft garden prunings, fallen leaves and annual weeds – though I deadhead these first in case the heap doesn't get hot enough to kill the seeds.

• **Perennial weeds** Though in theory the heat of the compost heap should kill them, it isn't worth taking risk of composting them. Other things to avoid are any diseased plant material; fish, meat or cooked food which can attract rodents; anything synthetic; cat or dog faeces; glossy magazines (that is, those printed on paper coated to make it shine); the top growth of potatoes, which often contains potato blight; large prunings from woody plants. For the sake of your hands, avoid anything barbed or thorny.

• **Trenching compost** If you don't have enough material to make much difference to the heap, bury kitchen and garden waste about 30 cm (12 in) deep in a trench, cover with soil and allow it to rot down for a few weeks. Plant greedy feeders like courgettes through this layer. This method of composting in a pit is ideal for hot countries without much rainfall.

## MULCHES

• **Composted bark** or wood shavings from factories are best used for paths.

• **Grass cuttings** are rich in nitrogen. They make a good mulch which can be used over newspaper to keep down weeds for short periods.

• **Mushroom compost** from commercial growers makes a good soil conditioner and mulch. Let it rot down. It contains chalk, so do not use it around acid-loving plants.

• **Seaweed** helps bind soil particles together and is rich in elements. It is good but expensive.

• **Spent hops** from a brewery add some nutrients and bulk to the soil.

• **Straw mulch** keeps the weeds at bay and slows down evaporation.

△ Straw mulch

△ Grass clipping mulch

△ Shredded bark mulch

◁ A thick mulch of straw round sweetcorn keeps the weeds at bay and slows down evaporation. It will eventually rot down and be taken down into the soil by worms, providing valuable humus.

## TYPES OF MANURE

A good pile of farmyard manure will make any gardener's eyes light up. It is wonderful both for soil texture and as a slow-release fertilizer. Some allotments get it in bulk. All manures need to be well rotted, either added to the compost or left in a heap for about six months until they break down and are sweet-smelling. They can then be forked into the soil for hungry feeders like potatoes or laid on top as a weed-preventing mulch to be gradually taken down by the worms. The most pleasant manures to handle are from horse, sheep and goat. Poultry manure is very strong, therefore best used as an activator in the compost heap and only sparingly mixed in with the soil. Cow and pig manures are effective but rather unpleasant to use, while rabbit and guinea pig droppings are pleasant and beneficial.

▽ Leafmould can be made in a cage of chicken wire. Simply collect up autumn leaves, place in the cage and allow to rot for 6 months to a year.

△ Winter tare is a good nitrogen-fixer and helps to prevent nutrients leaching out of the soil when the land is fallow through winter.

> ### *GARDENER'S TIP*
> *Leafmould does not provide much nourishment, but greatly improves the soil structure. Collect leaves in a cage of chicken wire. Add a little water and make a few holes in the sacks, then leave them for a season or two to rot.*

## GREEN MANURES

Green manures are fast-growing agricultural crops put in the ground for between six weeks and a year. When they are dug in they add to soil fertility. If you have empty beds which you are not ready to plant, a crop will make a temporary cover and help to keep the area free of weeds. Some green manures have root systems which will break up heavy ground, others store nitrogen in their roots which can be released to other plants. An overwintering crop protects the soil by holding in nutrients that might otherwise be leached by rain. The leaf cover gives shelter for useful predators of pests. Green manures are dug into the soil before they seed, usually a couple of weeks before the ground is needed. The

taller types are cut down and left to wilt before-hand. In a no-dig system, they can be hoed off and left on the surface. Buckwheat, clover and phacelia are good summer cover and have pretty flowers that attract friendly insects. So, if the land is ready to go but you don't want to plant it all at once, one of these would be a good solution.

• **Buckwheat** (*Fagopyrum esculentum*) is a tender annual, 90 cm (3 ft) high, a pretty plant in flower. Planted in late spring to grow through summer, it copes with poor soil and attracts hoverflies.

• **Crimson clover** (*Trifolium incarnatum*) is a hardy annual, 30 cm (12 in) high. Clover fixes nitrogen and is loved by bees. Plant it in spring to late summer and grow for two or three months, or leave over winter. It prefers light soils.

• **Fenugreek** (*Trigonella foenum-graecum*) is a semi-hardy annual, 60 cm (2 ft) high, a fast grower for summer. It forms bushy plants with weed-suppressing foliage. Plant in late spring or summer and grow for up to three months in well-drained but moisture-retentive soil.

• **Phacelia** (*Phacelia tanacetifolia*) is an annual, 90 cm (3 ft) high, with ferny leaves and bright blue flowers which are attractive to beneficial insects. Plant after the danger of frost is over and grow for a couple of months. It tolerates most soils.

• **Trefoil** (*Medicago lupulina*) is a biennial usu-ally treated as an annual, 30 cm (12 in) high, a nitrogen-fixing, low-growing plant that will cope with some shade and drought. Plant in the sum-mer to overwinter. It dislikes heavy acid soils.

• **Winter field beans** (*Vicia faba*) are an extremely hardy nitrogen fixer for the winter. Plant in late summer or early autumn. Avoid both waterlogging and drying out.

• **Winter tare** (*Vicia sativa*) is a hardy annual vetch, 75 cm (30 in) high, a fast-growing bushy plant that fixes nitrogen and makes good ground cover. Plant in late summer to overwinter. It dis-likes drought and prefers alkaline soils.

◁ Buckwheat.

△ Phacelia.

△ Crimson clover.

Aim for a rich diversity of plants. A monoculture, with row upon row of the same plant, is an invitation to pests who will see and smell it from afar. Provide camouflage with flowers and shrubs and include as great a variety of plants as possible.

# vegetables, herbs and flowers

◁ Sweet peas and Californian poppies growing together provide a vibrant splash of colour on this allotment.

# PLANTING
# schemes

Once you have divided up the space into areas for the different types of plants – vegetables, soft fruit, flowers and herbs – you are ready to make a planting plan and choose the varieties to suit your conditions.

- VEGETABLES IN ROTATION
  Potatoes
  Legumes
  Brassicas
  Root vegetables

- BLOCKS OR ROWS?
  Intercropping

- PLANTS FOR WILDLIFE

Produce is the priority of most allotment gardeners. Keep in mind the needs of your household and how much you will eat and enjoy or how much you may wish to give away. A common mistake is to plant far too much. If you are growing from seed, share the packet with others, or get your plants to the seedling stage and then trade them for others.

To enjoy your plot to the full, grow a few luxuries – asparagus, fine peas, artichokes, cherry tomatoes, mangetout peas, new potatoes, gourmet salad leaves, raspberries and strawberries. Try interesting heritage varieties from one of the seed libraries.

When deciding what to plant, always check the needs of the plants against your soil type – acid or alkaline – and their position in sun or shade, on damp or dry ground. Check the instructions on the seed packets.

△ A plot abundant with onions, potatoes and cabbages. The cabbages have been covered with fine netting to prevent cabbage moths and butterflies laying eggs.

◁ Purple sprouting broccoli

## VEGETABLES IN ROTATION

Rotation helps to prevent the build-up of diseases, increases soil fertility and makes cultivation easier and more economical. You need four or five separate beds and you should keep a record of what is planted in each one. The rotation groups are potatoes, legumes (peas and beans), brassicas (the cabbage family), and root vegetables which are moved round in a logical succession. The onion family, including leeks, garlic and shallots, can make a fifth bed.

• **Potatoes** are greedy and like heavily manured soil. The acidity in the manure will help to prevent potato scab. Incorporate plenty of it and add bone meal or fish, blood and bone meal for good measure and to add resistance.

• **Legumes** are the plants with pods – peas (among them the mangetout and sugar snap varieties) and all the beans. Legumes like rich soil, so the heavy manuring left from the potato crop the previous year is ideal. They don't like too much acidity, so apply some lime or calcified seaweed before planting. When harvesting, leave the roots of legumes in the soil, as they will be a valuable source of nitrogen for the following crop – the leafy brassicas. Pick the young pods regularly to encourage the growth of more.

• **Brassicas** are Brussels sprouts, cabbages (including Chinese cabbage), broccoli, cauliflower, calabrese, turnips, swedes and kohlrabi. The lime from the year before is beneficial against club root and the brassicas will enjoy the nitrogen left in the roots of the legumes. The tall sprouts and broccoli need firm soil, so don't disturb it too much by digging. Add some general fertilizer – blood, fish and bone or bone meal.

▽ Brussels sprouts keep going through the winter. Pick them from the bottom and remove yellowing leaves.

◁ Planting in blocks makes netting easier. The plants can be arranged quite close together so the plants fill out to shade out weeds.

▽ Sugar snap peas, caulliflower, beetroot and sweetcorn planted in traditional rows. Space has been left between rows to allow access to the plants. A mulching of straw or compost between rows would be advisable to keep the weeds down and help retain moisture.

• **Root vegetables** include the umbellifers and are chiefly carrots, parsnips, parsley, celery and celeriac and Florence fennel. The beetroot family, which includes beetroot, spinach, Swiss chard and spinach beet, make good bedfellows and, if you wish, tomatoes, marrows and courgettes can go in here too.

Either make a separate bed for onions, leeks, garlic and shallots or put them in here as well. Give the whole area a dressing of seaweed meal and treat each crop according to its needs.

## BLOCKS OR ROWS?

The traditional way of planting vegetables is in rows. It is the most practical method for beans, peas and other climbers. If the rows run from north to south they won't cast shade on each other. Climbers can also be grown up strings attached to a central pole, though there will be more of a shade problem in this arrangement. For other crops, try planting in rectangular blocks or squares. As the plants grow their leaves will spread together, shading out weeds and keeping in vital moisture. They will also be easier to manage when netting. In a block-shaped patch, it is just as easy to see which are crops and which are weeds.

**Intercropping** As you go along, make more use of the space and provide weed-suppressing cover by intercropping. In the little gaps between slow-growing plants, sow the seed of quick growers – salad leaves, oriental salad leaves or radishes. You can also use the space under tall plants like sweetcorn for low growers.

## PLANTS FOR WILDLIFE

Insects like simple flowers in which they can easily reach the nectar and pollen. Modern breeding has changed the shape of some flowers to such an extent that they are sometimes inaccessible to insects. Draw in hoverflies, ladybirds and lacewings, which are all useful for getting rid

◁ Clover growing under sweetcorn. The clover will retain moisture in the soil and can be dug into the soil as a green manure after the corn has been harvested.

△ Marigolds (Calendula) are planted to attract useful predators, such as hoverflies, ladybirds and lacewings, and will protect tomatoes from unwanted pests.

of pests, by planting marigolds *(Tagetes or Calendula)*, nasturtiums *(Tropaeolum)* and the poached-egg plant *(Limnanthes douglasii)*, fennel, angelica and dill. Bees, the pollinators, like a wide range of flowers, including those of vegetables and herbs, particularly mint, lavender and thyme.

Allow some flowers to go to seed to feed the birds through the winter. Berrying shrubs and trees and the hips of roses also provide food for them. Birds love fruit and although you will have to cover your fruit bushes to stop them stealing your crop, if you can find it in your heart to allow them some of the harvest, they will have a feast.

# DIRECTORY
# of vegetables

As a rough guide to planting vegetables, plant seed at a depth two and a half times the size of the seed. When seed is very fine, mix it with a little silver sand, sow it thinly on the surface and sprinkle compost over it.

- TRADITIONAL VEGETABLES
  A–Z directory
- ORIENTAL VEGETABLES
  A–Z directory

## TRADITIONAL VEGETABLES

*Abelmoschus esculentus*
### OKRA

Also called ladies' fingers or gumbo, okra is grown like tomatoes or aubergines. It needs a temperature of over 21°C (70°F) to do well. Either grow it in the greenhouse or, as it dislikes being moved, sow the seed outside when the weather is right and thin the seedlings to 45 cm (18 in) apart. Keep them on the dry side, but mulch them. They grow fast, and in warm countries you can get two crops in a summer.
**Problems:** The plants can irritate, so wear gloves when handling them.

**Pests and diseases:** Aphids pose the worst threat.
**Star variety:** F1 'Pure Luck'.

*Allium cepa*
### ONIONS and SHALLOTS

Onions and shallots can be grown from seed, which gives you a greater choice of varieties, but it is easier to cut down the work and buy onion or shallot 'sets' (small bulbs). The heat-treated ones are resistant to bolting. For medium-sized onions, plant the sets 5 cm (2 in) apart. If you want small onions plant them closer together; if you prefer larger ones, space the sets further apart.

△ Using spring, summer and winter types, cabbages can be grown all year round. They like to be rooted in solid ground.

Early Japanese varieties followed by a main crop mean that onions can be available all year. The Japanese ones are planted in late summer or autumn for eating in early summer; main-crop ones should be planted in spring. Rotation is important. Plant them in well-drained neutral to alkaline soil, no lower than pH 6.5. Add lime if the soil is too acid, with plenty of compost. Water the plants only in dry weather and keep them free of weeds. As they ripen, the leaves will bend away to allow the sun to mature the onions. Gently ease them apart with a fork, and about two weeks later lift them and leave them in the sun until the leaves are brown and the onions are ready to eat.

**Problems:** Sparrows like to pull the newly planted onions right out of the soil. Replant and protect them with fleece or netting.

**Pests and diseases:** Onion fly; mildew (downy mildew) in damp conditions.

**Star varieties:** Japanese 'Buffalo', main crop 'Golden Bear'.

*Allium porrum*
## LEEKS

Leeks are part of the winter scene of allotments. They can be left in the ground all through it and harvested when you want them. Start them either under cover or in a seed bed in spring. When you are ready to transplant them,

△ Onions ready for harvesting.

make a hole with a dibber 15 to 20 cm (6 to 8 in) deep, trim the roots if they are longer than this, then drop a leek into each hole and wash some soil over them with a watering can. Keep the plants free of weeds, and as they grow

either earth them up or drop sections of pipe over them to blanch the stems.

**Pests and diseases:** Few.

**Star variety:** 'Giant Winter – Catalina'.

*Allium sativum*
## GARLIC

Garlic should be planted in autumn or winter in free-draining soil. Buy a head of garlic from a garden centre and break into segments. Plant them upright with the tips just below the surface and 30 cm (12 in) apart in a sunny spot. Water only if the weather turns very dry, but keep free of weeds. The foliage comes up first and then dies down in summer. This is the time to dig up the bulbs. Dry them in the sun or a shed, and keep a couple to plant the following year.

**Pests and diseases:** Only a few: onion mildew, downy mildew.

▽ Leeks planted in a row.

*Apium graveolens* var*. dulce*
**CELERY**

Celery needs to grow fast in deep, well-drained, fairly alkaline soil with plenty of organic matter and water. The seeds can take a long time to germinate if the temperature is too warm, and the plants are likely to bolt if it's too low: 10°C (50°F) is about right. They are best planted under glass in spring. Self-blanching cultivars are the easiest. Scatter the seed on top of a pot of compost, leave it uncovered and prick out the seedlings as early as possible. Transplant them about 30 cm (12 in) apart when they have about six leaves. They work well planted in a block and will be ready to eat in late summer. For trench celery sow as above and when the seedlings are ready to be planted out, dig a trench 30 cm (12 in) deep and wider than that across, throw in rotted manure and soil and plant in a single row 30 cm (12 in) apart. When the plants are about 30 cm (12 in) tall, start to pile on more soil. Remove any side shoots, leaving single heads, and earth up the

△ Asparagus tips.

plants to about half their height. Add more earth every three weeks, and the celery will be ready to eat in midwinter.
**Pests and diseases:** Celery fly, carrot root fly, slugs.
**Star varieties:** Self-blanching 'Golden Self-blanching', trench 'Giant Pink – Mammoth Pink'.

*Apium graveolens* var. *rapaceum*
**CELERIAC**

Celeriac likes sun and rich soil with plenty of humus. Sow in mid spring at 18°C (65°F). Harden off the plants in a cold frame and, if the weather turns cold, delay them by clipping off the tops. Plant them out when it's warm with the crowns level with the soil, 30 cm (12 in) apart. Water them well and mulch. They will be ready in autumn but can be left in the ground until you want them. In chillier climates, cover them with straw when winter approaches.
**Pests and diseases:** Few.
**Star variety:** 'Monarch'.

*Asparagus officinalis*
**ASPARAGUS**

An asparagus bed lasts for twenty years. Buy one- to three-year-old male crowns as they produce fatter spears. The traditional bed is 1.2 m (4 ft) wide, with the crowns planted in two staggered rows 45 cm (18 in) apart. Dig a trench about a spit deep and weed it in spring. Asparagus will rot if it's too wet, so if you have heavy soil, add grit, manure and leaf mould to it, or raise the bed. If the soil is acid, add lime. Make a ridge of soil along the length of the trench and plant the crowns on top of it with the roots going downwards. When

△ Ruby chard stem.

you fill the trench the crowns should be about 15 cm (6 in) below ground. Don't cut any spears during the first year. Once established, asparagus can be harvested for six weeks in early summer and the remaining stalks left to grow. Cut them down when they turn yellow. In winter, give the bed a top dressing of rotted manure and sprinkle on some fertilizer the following spring.
**Problems:** Late frosts can spoil an early crop. Protect it with horticultural fleece.
**Pests and diseases:** Slugs, asparagus beetle, violet root rot.
**Star variety:** 'Connover's Colossal'.

*Beta vulgaris* subsp. *cicla*
**LEAF BEET**

Leaf beet (perpetual spinach, Swiss chard, silver beet, ruby chard or seakale beet) is an easily grown, cut-and-come-again crop that usually survives the winter and carries on the following year, when it goes to seed. All these varieties are colourful relations of beetroot and go with the brassicas. Sow in good, rich soil in a little shade in mid spring to early summer, then thin the seedlings to 30 cm (12 in) apart. Water them in dry spells. As they are maritime plants, feed with seaweed products. Keep harvesting by picking off the outer leaves when they are young.

**Pests and diseases:** Few: slugs, birds.

**Varieties:** Usually sold as perpetual spinach or spinach beet.

*Beta vulgaris* subsp. *vulgaris*
## BEETROOT

Beetroot can be eaten all summer if it is sown in batches every few weeks from spring. Usually the tapered varieties are used for the main crop. Sow in late summer and store for winter or leave in the ground. Beetroot grows in most soils with good drainage and full sun. Choose bolt-resistant varieties for the early crop. Plant clusters about 15 cm (6 in) apart, then thin to a single plant.

**Problems:** The roots will bleed if you cut into them with a hoe.

**Pests and diseases:** Only a few: leaf spot or mildew.

**Star varieties:** Round 'Boltardy', cylindrical 'Cheltenham Green Top'.

*Brassica napus* var. *napobrassica*
## SWEDES

Swedes go with other brassicas. Sow outside in early summer, 22.5 cm (9 in) apart. Mulch and keep them free of weeds. They can be left out through winter, but it is safer to lift and store them.

**Pests and diseases:** Club root, flea beetle, mildew, soft rot.

**Star variety:** 'Marian'.

△ Mature beetroot plant.

*Brassica oleracea*
## CALABRESE

Calabrese is an annual which is eaten in summer. It likes a well-drained sunny site with plenty of humus. Start under glass or sow seed outside from spring, spacing three seeds at 'stations' 20 cm (8 in) apart and thinning to a single plant later. Water plentifully in dry weather.

**Pests and diseases:** Cabbage root fly, cabbage moth, cabbage butterflies, club root, pigeons.

**Star variety:** 'Shogun'.

*Brassica oleracea*
## KALE

Also called curly kale, it should be planted in a nursery bed in spring. Thin seedlings and transplant them, 45 cm (18 in) apart, in mid to late summer. Keep watered and harvest in autumn.

**Pests and diseases:** Club root, cabbage root fly, cabbage moth, cabbage butterflies, birds.

**Star variety:** 'Fribor'.

*Brassica oleracea*
## CAULIFLOWERS

Cauliflowers are temperamental. They have a tendency to flower before they are ready to eat (premature 'curding'), and lack of water or nutrients can spoil them. Seeds can come up 'blind', that is without a central bud. The heads or 'curds' must be kept out of direct sun-light and need to be covered with their leaves. They dislike being transplanted or placed in loose soil. The autumn and winter types are much like broccoli. Start with the summer ones. Sow them outdoors in rich, moist, firm soil, out of the wind. Follow the timing instructions on the seed packet. Space them about 60 cm (2 ft) apart.

**Pests and diseases:** Cabbage butterfly, cabbage moth, cabbage root fly, club root.

**Star varieties:** Summer 'Alpha 5 – Polaris', autumn or winter F1 'Castlegrant'.

△ A cauliflower ready to eat.

*Brassica oleracea* Capitata Group
**CABBAGES**

Cabbages can be grown all year. They like to be rooted in solid ground, so tread in firmly. Winter cabbage should be sown in spring in shallow drills 15 cm (6 in) apart in a seed bed. Transplant to final positions 45 cm (18 in) apart in midsummer. Harvest when the heads are firm from autumn. Treat spring cabbage like winter cabbage but sow it in late summer. Sow summer cabbage in late winter in seed trays under glass. Harden off the seedlings and plant 45 cm (18 in) apart under cloches in early spring.
**Pests and diseases:** Club root, cabbage root fly, caterpillars, cabbage butterfly, mealy aphids, cabbage whitefly.
**Star varieties:** Winter 'January King 3', spring 'Offenham 1 Myatt's Offenham Compacta', summer F1 'Hispa'.

△ Ball-headed cabbages.

*Brassica oleracea* Gemmifera Group
**BRUSSELS SPROUTS**

Sprouts are slow growers. Plant them in shallow drills from early to mid spring in a seed bed and cover with netting to protect them from the birds. When they are 5 to 7.5 cm (2 to 3 in) tall transplant them to a wider spacing of 75 cm (2.6 ft). Keep them free of weeds, well mulched and watered. Support the tall varieties. Remove yellowing leaves at the base and harvest from the bottom of the plants upwards from autumn to spring. Dig out the whole plants at the end of the season.
**Pests and diseases:** Club root, cabbage root fly, cabbage moth, cabbage butterflies, birds.
**Star varieties:** F1 'Cascade'. F1 'Oliver'.

*Brassica oleracea* Gongylodes Group
**KOHLRABI**

Kohlrabi is popular in Eastern Europe as a substitute for turnips. Sow the seed outside in the brassica patch when the soil temperature is above 10°C (50°F) and thin to 20 cm (8 in) apart. Water only if they are wilting. Kohlrabi doesn't keep as well as turnips, so use shortly after harvesting.
**Pests and diseases:** Few.
**Star variety:** 'Rowel'.

*Brassica oleracea* Italica Group
**SPROUTING BROCCOLI**

This is a winter crop, with the best in early spring. Sow seeds late in spring 15 cm (6 in) apart in a seed bed and transplant them to their final positions 75 cm (2.5 ft) apart when they are large enough. Cultivate them as you

△ A mature kohlrabi plant.

would calabrese, and keep picking to encourage fresh, new growth.
**Pests and diseases:** Cabbage root, cabbage moth, cabbage butterflies, club root, pigeons.
**Star variety:** 'Early Purple Sprouting Improved'.

*Brassica rapa* Rapifera Group
**TURNIPS**

Turnips can be harvested through summer and autumn and stored for winter. The soil should be neither too acid nor too dry, and worked to a fine tilth. Summer plantings are happy in light shade. Thin to 10 cm (4 in) apart. Plant at three-week intervals outside after the soil has warmed up, for cold will make them bolt. Cover them with cloches and water in dry periods.
Pests and diseases: Flea beetle.
Star variety: 'Golden Ball'.

*Capsicum annuum*
**PEPPERS** and **CHILLIES**

Both sweet peppers or bell peppers, and chillies or hot peppers, are tropical plants needing rich, moist, slightly acid soil and sunshine, but they can be grown in temperate climates in the same way as tomatoes. Start them off in a greenhouse. Plant them out under cloches when the soil is warm, spacing them quite far apart, 35 cm (14 in), to allow air to circulate. Stake them. To encourage the plants to be sturdy enough to bear the weight of the fruits, pinch out the growing tips when they are about 30 cm (12 in) high. Water them often without letting them get too wet, and feed them with liquid fertilizer once a week. Chilli plants are prolific. A couple of plants will give you plenty for one season.

**Pests and diseases:** Botrytis, red spider mite, whitefly, aphids.

**Star varieties:** Pepper 'Beauty Bell', chilli 'Harabero'.

*Cichorium intybus*
## CHICORY, RADICCHIO and ENDIVE
Chicory is either the white shoot or 'chicon' of 'forcing chicory' or a 'non-forcing' type which is grown like lettuce in summer. Forcing chicory is planted outside in the summer. Sow it sparingly in finely raked soil and thin the seedlings to 22.5 cm (9 in) apart. The plants like fertile soil and sunshine. Water until the seedlings come up, then leave them fairly dry to encourage root growth. Dig them up in late autumn or early winter, cut the leaves off just above the crown, trim the roots to about 30 cm (12 in) and store in sand in a frost-free shed. When you want some chicons, plant them in large pots of moist soil with the crowns just showing.

△ Red chilli pepper.

Keep the pots in the dark at a temperature no less than 10°C (50°F) and the chicons will grow in about three weeks. If they are broken off carefully, more will form. Treat non-forcing chicory in the same way to begin with, but keep up the watering and harvest in late summer. Some kinds are self-blanching. If yours are not, put a flower-pot (with its hole blocked) over the centre of each plant and keep them dry under a cloche for the last week or ten days before picking the leaves.

**Pests and diseases:** Few: cutworm, wireworm, slugs.

**Star varieties:** Forcing 'Brussels Witloof', non-forcing 'Rossa di Verona' (radicchio), 'Sugar Loaf' (bright green), naturally blanched.

▷ Miniature cucumbers ready for picking. This plant has been trained up a string.

*Cucumis sativus*
## CUCUMBERS
Cucumbers should be started indoors in cooler countries, where the outdoor, 'ridge' types are the best proposition, especially some of the new varieties. Plant a couple of seeds in each pot in spring, then choose the stronger of each pair and plant them out after the danger of frost is over. If seeds are sown outside, cover them with a cloche. They like rich, moisture-retentive soil. Make a slight mound and plant three seeds in each position, thinning them later. Never let them dry out. Growing them up canes avoids slugs.

**Pests and diseases:** Cucumber mosaic virus, slugs.

**Star variety:** F1 'Bush Champion'.

*Cucurbita pepo*
## COURGETTES and MARROWS

These are prolific and easy, given plenty of water. Sow them indoors in late spring or early summer, one seed to a pot, or wait till midsummer and plant them outside in well-manured soil 90 to 120 cm (3 to 4 ft) apart. Plunge a section of pipe into the soil to get water to the roots. Grow the plants on a tripod or select bush types. The more courgettes you harvest, the more you will get, and if you leave them they will grow into marrows. The flowers are edible.

**Pests and diseases:** Slugs, aphids, mildew, cucumber mosaic virus.

**Star variety:** F1 'Defender'.

△ Globe artichoke.

*Cynara cardunculus* Scolymus Group
## GLOBE ARTICHOKES

These are easily grown from rooted off-sets, planted 1.2 m (4 ft) apart just below the surface outside in a sunny position in spring. They dislike cold and damp. Water them well in their first year. Protect them against cold in winter with straw. Mulch and manure in spring, and divide them every three years. Cardoons *(Cynara cardunculus)* are similar, though the stalks are eaten, not the flower buds.

**Pests and diseases:** Resistant to most, except aphids.

**Star varieties:** Artichoke 'Green Globe', cardoon 'Gigante di Romana'.

*Daucus carota* subsp. *sativus*
## CARROTS

Carrots need a light, free-draining, fertile soil. If your soil is heavy, grow

◁ A marrow ready for harvesting.

them in raised beds. Sow a few seeds outdoors every two weeks from mid spring (earlier if you are using cloches) and you'll have a succession of carrots until early winter. Sow seed as sparsely as possible, mixing it with silver sand. Water the plants in dry periods.

**Pests and diseases:** Carrot fly.

**Star varieties:** 'Flyaway', 'Autumn King'.

*Eruca vesicaria*
## ROCKET

Rocket is expensive to buy but easy to grow. Scatter a few seeds from spring on and cut the plants when they are 7.5 to 10 cm (3 to 4 in) high. They spring up again and survive mild winters.

**Pests and diseases:** Flea beetle.

*Foeniculum vulgare* var. *dulce*
## FLORENCE FENNEL

Unlike the herb fennel, this is grown for its aniseed-tasting bulb. It needs plenty of moisture, sunshine and good, rich soil. Sow outside in small batches from spring. Thin to 30 cm (12 in) apart and keep well watered to prevent bolting.

**Pests and diseases:** Slugs.

**Star variety:** 'Perfection'.

*Helianthus tuberosus*
## JERUSALEM ARTICHOKES

These are easy, hardy and may become rampant. Buy a few tubers from a greengrocer and plant them in spring 10 to 15 cm (4 to 6 in) apart in fine sandy soil. Harvest the tubers a month after flowering or after frost has killed off the tops. Clear the ground in spring and start again.

**Pests and diseases:** Slugs, sclerotinia.

**Star variety:** 'Black Beauty'.

*Lactuca sativa*

## LETTUCE

Including Cos, loose-leaf kinds (among them designer leaves like Lollo Rosso), butterheads and crispheads, lettuce can be grown outside from spring till autumn. For a continuous supply sow a few seeds every fortnight from mid spring to midsummer, or earlier if you are growing under cover. If you protect them against frost with cloches, a cold frame or a greenhouse, you can grow them through the winter too. Lettuce likes a coolish spot, partly shaded in the heat of summer. Sow the seed in moisture-retentive soil and thin the seedlings to about 15 cm (6 in) apart for the smaller types. Keep them watered.

**Problems:** They can be slow to germinate in hot weather and have a tendency to bolt.

**Pests and diseases:** Slugs, aphids (lettuce root aphid), cut worm, grey mould, birds.

△ 'Cocarde' lettuce is a cut-and-come-again variety.

**Star varieties:** Oak-leaf 'Red Salad Bowl', cut-and-come-again 'Cocarde', Cos 'Lobjoit's Green Cos', winter 'Parella Green'.

*Lycopersicon esculentum*

## TOMATOES

Tomatoes don't need pruning if you choose bush types. Either buy a few young plants or raise them from seed in a propagator in the middle of spring at 19°C (65°F). Harden off the seedlings carefully and plant outside in a sunny and sheltered spot in early summer. Set climbing types 45 cm (18 in) apart and bush ones 60 cm (24 in). Mulch them and cover with fleece or cloches. They like rich, well-drained but moisture-retentive soil and are often raised in grow-bags. They need frequent watering and a weekly feed. Liquid comfrey is particularly good.

◁ 'Shirley' tomatoes.

**Pests and diseases:** Whitefly, greenfly, spider mite, leaf mould, tomato blight, virus, slugs, birds.

**Star varieties:** 'Alicante', 'Gardener's Delight'.

*Pastinaca sativa*

## PARSNIPS

These are very hardy. They need a rich soil cleared of stones, though you can get away with filling individual holes with compost if the soil is poor. Plant about three seeds in each 'station' in late spring, then thin out, keeping the strongest. Spacing depends on the variety and ranges from 7.5 to 15 cm (3 to 6 in). Keep them weeded. Don't overwater as this will encourage leaves rather than roots. Harvest them in autumn and through the winter.

Problems: Germination can be slow.

**Pests and diseases:** Carrot root fly, parsnip canker, birds.

**Star variety:** 'Tender and True'.

### *Phaseolus coccineus*
### RUNNER BEANS

Runner beans should be sown outside in rich, moist soil once the danger of frost has passed in late spring. They like a cool, damp root-run, so add plenty of humus and mulch. Plant 15 cm (6 in) apart with 60 cm (2 ft) between rows in a sheltered place. They need strong supports about 3 m (10 ft) high, such as a line of crossed poles.

Problems: They can be slow to produce a crop in hot weather.

**Pests and diseases:** Only a few: mice, slugs.

**Star variety:** 'Enorma'.

### *Phaseolus lunatus*
### LIMA BEANS

Also known as butter beans, these grow only in warm climates. Sow in late spring under glass or outside when the soil temperature is over 18°C (65°F), 60 cm (2 ft) apart. Plant half a dozen seeds in each 'station' and thin to three once they have germinated. Mulch well.

**Pests and diseases:** Aphids, pea or bean weevils.

**Star variety:** 'King of the Garden'.

### *Phaseolus vulgaris*
### FRENCH BEANS

Also known as dwarf, string or snap beans, these like warm, slightly acid soil. In cool climates either start them under glass in mid spring or plant them outside in early summer in a protected, sunny spot. Prepare the ground well and add plenty of compost so the roots don't dry out. Sow 20 cm (8 in) apart. The climbing varieties need support. Pinch out the growing tips when the plants reach the top of their sticks. Mulch and water them in dry periods.

**Pests and diseases:** Slugs, aphids, halo blight.

**Star varieties:** Dwarf bean 'Sprite', Climbing bean 'Hunter'.

△ Mangetout peas.

### *Pisum sativum*
### PEAS, MANGETOUT, SUGAR SNAPS

Peas do best in cool conditions in light alkaline soil with plenty of moisture. The overwintering types are generally disappointing. It is far better to plant peas in spring when the soil is warm, at the same time as mangetout and sugar snap varieties. Plant them in a drill about 5 to 7.5 cm (2 to 3 in) apart and cover with cloches. The 'semi-leafless' peas will support each other, but other kinds need some framework. Net them against birds. The more you pick the more will grow. When the crop is finished, leave the roots in the ground.

**Pests and diseases:** Pea moths, pea and bean weevils, mildew, birds, mice.

**Star varieties:** Early 'Early Onward', late 'Hurst Greenshaft', mangetout 'Oregon Sugar Pod', sugar snap 'Mammouth Melting Sugarpod'.

△ Beans growing up canes.

*Raphanus sativus*
## RADISHES

Radishes should be sown little and often in llight sandy soil from spring on. There are types with red or black skins and winter varieties which are sown in late summer and can be harvested over a long period.

**Pests and diseases:** Flea beetle.
**Star varieties:** Summer 'French Breakfast', winter 'Black Spanish Round'.

*Rheum x cultorum*
## RHUBARB

This is a reliable, easy crop. Buy a crown or persuade a friend to give you a piece. Mix plenty of humus into the soil, and lime if it is acid, and plant the cuttings when they are dormant in a sunny spot 2.5 cm (1 in) deep and 90 cm (3 ft) apart. Keep them well watered but not

△ Mature radish plants.

waterlogged. Harvest the stalks in their second year from spring through to autumn, always leaving three or four stems with leaves. Then allow the plant to build up again for the following year. Pile on plenty of manure in the autumn.
**Pests and diseases:** Few.

*Scorzonera hispanica*
## SCORZONERA
see *Tragopogon porrifolius* **SALSIFY**.

*Solanum melongena*
## AUBERGINES

These are grown like tomatoes. In cooler countries, sow seed under glass in spring. The plants will survive outside only if placed in a sheltered, sunny spot in summer under the protection of a cloche. They need well-drained and manured soil with a high potash content and plenty of water. Feed them when the fruits are developing.
**Pests and diseases:** Whitefly, greenfly, red spider mite, botrytis.
**Star variety:** 'Black Beauty'.

*Solanum tuberosum*
## POTATOES

Potatoes like plenty of humus and moisture, and prefer a sandy, acid soil. Dig over the patch in the autumn and incorporate lots of manure or compost. Buy disease-free seed potatoes early in spring. Put them in a cool, light place to sprout. Plant the early ones a month before the last frosts, adding a general fertilizer. Make a drill about 15 cm (6 in) deep and plant the potatoes 40 cm (16 in) apart. They need to be earthed up about three times to encourage growth and prevent poisonous green patches from developing. As an alternative to earthing up, plant them through slits in a covering of black plastic. The main-crop ones go in at the same time with a wider spacing of 75 cm (2.5 ft). Start to lift the early ones when they flower, but leave the main crop until the autumn.
**Pests and diseases:** Potato blight, scab, slugs, wireworms.
**Star varieties:** Early 'Concorde', main crop 'Avalanche'.

△ Ripened aubergines.

*Spinacea oleracea*

## SPINACH

Spinach needs plenty of water and shade. The first crops can be grown inside late in winter at 18°C (65°F) to be planted out early in spring under cloches 15 cm (6 in) apart in rich moist soil on the acid side (pH 6.5-7). For a constant supply plant a few seeds every two weeks outside through summer. Plant in late summer for winter crops. If you harvest the outside leaves the spinach will continue to grow.

**Problems:** Bolting; New Zealand spinach *(Tetragonia expansa)* and spinach beet *(Beta vulgaris* subsp. *cicla)* are less prone to this rapid growth.

**Pests and diseases:** Fairly resistant. Aphids, downy mildew.

**Star variety:** Summer 'Atlanta'.

*Tragopogon porrifolius*

## SALSIFY

Salsify and Scorzonera (Scorzonera hispanica) are slow-growing root vegetables popular in Southern Europe. They are similar, though the first has white skin, the second black. The young shoots and flower buds can be cooked like asparagus, and the flowers attract useful predators. Sow in spring about 30 cm (12 in) apart in soil that is not too rich. The roots are ready in autumn, but can be left over winter.

**Pests and diseases:** Few. Carrot fly.

**Star varieties:** Salsify 'Sandwich Island Mammouth', scorzonera 'Long Black Maximum'.

*Valerianella locusta*

## CORN SALAD

Also known as lamb's lettuce, this is a

△ Sweetcorn growing in a block to help wind pollination.

useful salad for winter. Sow in late summer in rich well-drained soil and thin the plants to 15 cm (6 in) apart. Harvest through the winter, picking single leaves for a cut-and-come-again crop.

**Pests and diseases:** Generally trouble-free.

**Star variety:** 'Vit'.

*Vicia faba*

## BROAD BEANS

These are easy and hardy. They can be planted in late autumn for an early crop, followed by a main-crop sowing in early spring. If they are picked young, the entire pod can be eaten. Tall varieties need support. Plant the seeds about 22.5 cm (9 in) apart in slightly acid soil (pH 6.5). Cover overwintering crops with fleece. In warmer climates these beans will grow again and give a second crop if they are cut back to near the base.

**Pests and diseases:** Pea and bean weevil, chocolate spot.

**Star varieties:** Autumn 'Aquadulce Claudia', spring 'Express'.

*Zea mays*

## SWEETCORN

This is one vegetable which is far more delicious when cooked absolutely fresh. It needs a warm, sheltered site, protection from winds and soil on the acid side. In cooler countries sow seeds individually in pots indoors in spring. Harden the seedlings off well and then transplant them outside when the soil is warm. As they are wind pollinated, they are best planted in a block about 35 cm (15 in) apart to encourage this. Water generously when they are in flower and when the kernels are swelling to improve the crop. Look out for the new supersweet cultivars.

**Pests and diseases:** Resistant to most, except mice.

**Star variety:** 'Early Extra Sweet'.

## ORIENTAL VEGETABLES

These Chinese or Japanese plants grow fast and need lots of water. Some of them are summer salads of the cut-and-come-again type, and some will survive winter. Any fertile soil will do, but oriental brassicas have a tendency to bolt if the temperatures are too low at the early stages of growth or if they become stressed. With the exception of Chinese cabbage (which is the target of all the usual pests and diseases of cabbages) they are resistant to most pests, though attractive to slugs. The choice of seed is somewhat limited in the West.

*Brassica juncea*

### CHINESE MUSTARD GREENS

These should be sown in late summer or autumn. Pick the leaves through the winter and harvest finally in spring. 'Green in Snow' (a winter green) and 'Red Giant' (a pungent red cabbage which can be chopped into salads) are the easiest to obtain in the West.

*Brassica oleracea* Alboglabra Group

### CHINESE BROCCOLI or KALE

This can take both heat and some frost. Sow it in midsummer and eat young leaves or overwinter it.

*Brassica rapa*

### CHINESE CABBAGE, CHOP SUEY GREENS

Cylindrical, hearted or loose-leaved, Chinese cabbage should be planted with other brassicas in a shady spot. Chop suey greens are grown in hot countries as a winter crop and in cooler ones outdoors in summer. They are a good catch crop for spring. Leaves and petals can be used in salads or stir-fries.

*Brassica rapa* Chinensis Group

### PAK CHOI

This is the most familiar of the Chinese cabbages and can be eaten two to eight weeks after planting outside in summer or under glass in late spring.

*Brassica rapa* var. *nipposinica*

### JAPANESE GREENS or MIZUNA

This can cope with almost any extreme except drought. The leaves make good off-season salad and the white stalks can be cooked. Plant outside and grow under cloches through the winter in temperate climates.

△ Pak choi.

△ 'Red Giant' mustard greens.

# DIRECTORY OF HERBS
# and flowers

Break with allotment tradition by planting aromatic Mediterranean herbs and growing your favourite flowers among the vegetables. You will be helping wildlife by bringing in birds, bees and helpful insects to keep the ecology going.

- PERENNIAL HERBS
  A–Z directory

- ANNUAL and BIENNIAL HERBS
  A–Z directory

- FLOWERS

△ Remove fennel flowers to prevent seeding.

## PERENNIAL HERBS

Shrubby perennials, including rosemary, sage, lavender, thyme and winter savory, need a sunny spot with good drainage. Add grit to the soil if necessary. Buy small plants or propagate from cuttings. Hardy perennials, including chives, tarragon and mint, will die back in winter and grow again next year.

- *Allium schoenoprasum* **CHIVES** like moist soil and can take some shade. The easiest method to start them off is to ask someone to give you a few small bulbs from an established plant. Lift the clump every three years, split it and replant the sections in fresh soil.

△ Mixing in flowers among the vegetables in the cottage garden style promotes biodiversity in an allotment.

- *Artemisia dracunculus* **FRENCH TARRAGON** can only be grown from cuttings. It needs full sun and good drainage. Divide every few years to keep the potent flavour. Russian or false tarragon (Artemisia dracunculoides) is grown from seed and is bigger and more hardy than the French variety, but is inferior in flavour and less sought after by cooks.

- *Foeniculum vulgare* **FENNEL** will scatter its seeds everywhere unless

△ Rosemary, a perennial herb.

you remove the flower heads, and it will cross-pollinate with coriander and dill. Sow a few seeds in spring or autumn, 60 cm (2 ft) apart, outside in a sunny spot in fertile soil, or persuade a friend to give you a piece of root from an established plant.

• *Mentha* species **MINTS** come from a number of species and varieties, and most of them will spread rapidly unless they are prevented. There are dozens of different sorts, with scents or flavours ranging from eau de cologne to ginger. Grow the plants in a container, or sink one with its bottom removed into the ground.

• *Origanum majorana* **SWEET MARJORAM** is the best kind for cooking. It is a shrubby perennial which is usually grown as an annual in cool climates. Either buy plants or sow seed outside in late spring.

• *Rumex acetosa* **SORREL** is another determined spreader. Sow it in spring in any well-drained soil.

▷ Sweet peas supported by bean canes.

## ANNUALS AND BIENNIAL HERBS

• *Anethum graveolens* **DILL** needs well-drained soil and sun. Its leaves are so fine that it takes a number of plants to provide a fair quantity. Sow seed in batches from spring, inside or outside.

• *Borago officinalis* **BORAGE** is a must for bees and has cornflower blue flowers which are good in salads. Sow seed in spring outside.

• *Coriandrum sativum* **CORIANDER** is another candidate for good drainage and sunshine. You need quite a few plants to get enough leaves. Sow in small batches from spring, inside or outside.

• *Ocimum basilicum* **BASIL** is a tender annual and in cooler countries can be grown outside only during the summer, though it grows quite well in pots inside too. The leaves of purple basil are just as aromatic as the green.

• *Petroselinum crispum* **PARSLEY** can be slow to germinate and is best raised indoors and transplanted into rich, moist soil worked to a fine tilth.

△ Gladioli and cacti in a Mexican allotment.

## FLOWERS

Dahlias, chrysanthemums and sweet peas are traditional allotment flowers, but if you want to grow flowers for the house the range can be extended greatly. The easiest to grow are bulbs for spring and autumn and hardy annuals for the summer. They can be sown outside after the danger of frost is past. Look for varieties that are long-lasting and don't flop when the flowers have been picked.

Growing fruit is far less arduous than growing vegetables, and just as rewarding. Many people say that the raspberry crop alone pays the rent for their allotment. Once planted, fruit more or less looks after itself and will yield for years.

# fruit

4

## GROWING SOFT FRUIT
Strawberries
Gooseberries
Blackcurrants
Redcurrants and whitecurrants
Raspberries
Loganberries and blackberries
Blueberries

## GROWING FRUIT TREES
Choosing trees
How to prune
Planting fruit trees
**PROJECT** – *Making a cordon*

◁ A small vineyard has been planted on this plot.

# GROWING SOFT
# fruit

**Buy plants from a reliable nursery, if possible with a virus-free certificate. Virus disease is the only real threat to soft fruit. With this in mind, don't put new plants where soft fruit has been before, and water all soft fruit at the base. Birds will strip your fruit crops so netting is essential.**

- STRAWBERRIES
- GOOSEBERRIES
- BLACKCURRANTS
- REDCURRANTS AND WHITECURRANTS
- RASPBERRIES
- LOGANBERRIES AND BLACKBERRIES
- BLUEBERRIES

*Fragaria x ananassa*
## STRAWBERRIES

Strawberries are usually started from rooted runners in fresh ground every three years. Buy virus-free stock and plant the runners in late summer in rich, moist but well-draining soil in an airy but sunny spot. Make sure that the crowns (where the roots join the tops) are at soil level. Space them about 45 cm (18 in) apart. Either plant through a membrane (or a layer of black plastic) or lay straw under the fruits as they form to prevent them getting muddy and to deter slugs. Use netting or cloches to keep the birds off. After cropping, cut off the old leaves and cut back the plants to 10 cm (4 in). Remove the runners unless you want to propagate them. If you do, plant them in pots next to the parent plants and peg them down with a hairpin of wire until they root and you can separate them.
**Pest and diseases:** Slugs, birds, grey mould (botrytis), worst in wet summers, **Star variety:** 'Rhapsody'.

*Ribes grossularia*
## GOOSEBERRIES

Gooseberry bushes bear fruit for some twenty years and are the earliest soft fruits. They can suffer from frost and they don't care to be toasted. They

△ Letting the fruits ripen on a bed of straw keeps them clean and helps to deter unwanted slugs.

aren't fussy about soil, are not prone to virus diseases and they don't mind a little shade. They can be grown as bushes, trained as a fruit fence or made into a mop-headed standard, though these need staking as they become top-heavy. Buy two- or three-year-old plants with clear stems 10 to 15 cm (4 to 6 in) long. Plant them during the dormant season with plenty of well-rotted organic matter and mulch. If you are growing them as bushes, prune

△ 'Spinefree' gooseberries.

after harvest, aiming for a balanced and open goblet shape. Keep the stem clear to 10 to 15 cm (4 to 6 in) by cutting off any new side shoots. Prune the leader back to half of its new growth every year so that the plant makes strong side branches to support the fruit. As plants are established, reduce the length of these branches by a third after harvest.

**Pests and diseases:** Mildew (American gooseberry mildew).

**Star variety:** 'Invicta'.

*Ribes nigrum*

## BLACKCURRANTS

These are long-lived and make big bushes about 1.5 to 1.8 m (5 to 6 ft) high, though compact forms are available. Buy bare-rooted two-year-old plants. They like an open, sunny and sheltered position but can stand some shade. They need a good depth of soil for their roots to spread and should be planted 5 cm (2 in) deeper than they were when bought, with plenty of compost. Plant in autumn or in the dormant season and cut back the shoots to near ground level. Pile on organic matter as a mulch to keep in moisture. Water them in dry spells. This year's shoots will bear fruit next year. After fruiting, prune out any weak or broken growths 2.5 cm (1 in) from the ground. When the bush is established, cut out one third of the wood after leaf fall in autumn.

**Pests and diseases:** Blackcurrant gall mite, aphids.

**Star variety:** 'Ben Sarek'.

△ Blackcurrants.

◁ Horticultural membrane is good for keeping strawberries clean and will deter both weeds and slugs.

*Ribes sativum*

## REDCURRANTS and WHITECURRRANTS

Both tolerate partial shade. They don't need as rich a soil as the other soft fruits. As they flower early, find them a sheltered spot. They are usually grown as bushes but can be trained in other ways. Plant during the dormant season, preferably in autumn when the soil is still warm, and mulch. As with gooseberries, keep the stem clear of side branches to10 cm (4 in). When pruning, aim for an airy goblet shape with about eight or ten branches and remove any suckers. Once established, cut the new growth back to about five leaves after fruiting. No virus-free certificate is available for these currants, so rely on a good nursery to provide healthy stock.

**Pests and diseases:** Coral spot, aphids.
**Star varieties:** Redcurrant 'Red Lake', whitecurrant 'White Grape'.

△ 'White Versailles' whitecurrants.

△ Redcurrants ready for picking.

*Rubus idaeus*

## RASPBERRIES should crop for a
good twelve years, if they don't get a virus, and you can extend the season by planting both summer- and autumn-fruiting varieties.

**• Summer-fruiting raspberries**
produce fresh canes each year which bear fruit the following year, before dying off and being replaced by new ones. They flower in late spring and like a protected sunny position (though they will take a little shade) and a well-drained site with slightly acid soil (pH 6.5–6.7). Plant in early autumn or through the winter. Dig a trench one spit deep, and put in plenty of well-rotted manure or compost. If you are worried

△ Raspberries fruit in summer or autumn.

about drainage, you can raise the bed. The canes will need supports and the traditional method is posts and wire. Plant the canes 5 to 7.5 cm (2 to 3 in) deep, spreading out the roots. Cut each cane above a bud about 30 cm (12 in) high. Water and mulch.

Control the weeds, being careful not to damage the roots which are close to the surface. Remove flowers in the first season so that the plant concentrates on making strong canes. Tie in about seven canes on each plant and cut down the others to ground level. Water in dry periods. In the second summer cut down the canes that have fruited. Select seven of the strongest new ones to tie in for the following year's fruit.

### • Autumn-fruiting raspberries

don't need support and do their growing and fruiting in a single year. Plant in early autumn or through the winter and prune and space them in the same way as the summer ones. Cut off all the canes to ground level in late winter.

**Pests and diseases:** Raspberry beetle, aphids.

**Star varieties:** Summer-fruiting 'Glen Moy', 'Autumn Bliss'.

### *Rubus loganobaccus, R. ulmifolius*
### LOGANBERRIES and
### BLACKBERRIES

Loganberries, blackberries and their hybrids like tayberries, boysenberries, youngberries and others, are briar fruits that follow the early raspberries. Plant them in the winter months, 3 m (10 ft) apart in deep, well-prepared, moist, slightly acid soil (pH5.6–6) and cut them down to a bud about 22.5 cm (9 in) above the ground. They like sun but can

take partial shade. They need strong supports 3 m (10 ft) tall, traditionally made of post and wire. There are thornless varieties which make training easier. Tie in as they grow to stop them tangling. They flower and fruit on one-year-old wood. A simple way to train them is to keep last season's wood on one side and the new season's on the other. After fruiting, cut down old canes to ground level and tie in the new ones.

**Pests and diseases:** Raspberry beetle, aphids.

**Star variety:** Blackberry 'Fantasia'.

### *Vaccinium corymbosum*
### BLUEBERRIES

These are popular in the US and like lots of moisture and extremely acid soil. Unless you have this, grow them in

large pots in ericaceous (lime-free) compost and water them with rain water. 'High bush' blueberries are the best variety for fruit. Blueberries need to be pollinated by separate plants so grow two different varieties which flower at the same time close to each other. Plant two- or three-year-old bushes in the dormant season. They take three to eight years to fruit, but then they produce abundant crops. Prune them in winter, cutting out about one third of the old or damaged wood down to its base, and trim off the tops in spring to keep the bushes in neat shapes.

**Pests and diseases:** Few.

**Star variety:** 'Bluecrop'.

▽ Blueberries produce abundant crops.

# GROWING FRUIT
## trees

Allotment sites often ban trees as they can take up too much room and shade other plots. However, many sites will allow dwarf fruit trees or a fruit fence of cordons or espaliers. Small fruit trees are a good extra dimension for wildlife and they will fruit for years, needing little care.

- CHOOSING TREES
- HOW TO PRUNE
- PLANTING FRUIT TREES
- **PROJECT ~ *Making a cordon***

## CHOOSING TREES

If you plan to plant only one tree choose a self-pollinator on the right-sized root stock. The staff of a good nursery will advise you. A half-standard tree has a trunk up to 1.2 m (4 ft) tall, the size you see most often in gardens. You can buy a bush tree (M.27 is very dwarf and M.9 a little larger) which can be grown in a large pot or barrel, or a bigger one (M.26 or the slightly larger M.106), which is the right size for cordons and espaliers.

## HOW TO PRUNE

Pruning is an art and a skill to be refined over the years. Remember, though, that in nature nothing is pruned and plants survive. The main purpose is to cut out dead and crossing branches for the health of the tree, to manipulate it to increase the yield of fruit, and to shape it as you wish. In the first few years the aim is to make a balanced framework and to let light and air through to the middle in an open goblet shape. Make sure the tree is balanced and that there is only one strong leader – forked leaders will put strain on the tree later. If you want plants to become bushier, take out the terminal (topmost) bud, which encourages side branches to grow. Always use sharp tools that are up to the job and cut just above a node or bud pointing in the direction you want the branch to grow to avoid die-back. Trees are generally pruned in the dormant season to encourage growth. However, dwarf trained forms are pruned in summer. This has the opposite effect, which is to keep them compact.

△ It is possible to buy tiny trees on dwarf rootstocks, such as M.27. Such trees will still produce a good crop of fruit.

△ Apples growing on an allotment.

**PLANTING FRUIT TREES**
The old saying, 'spend one sou on the plant then twenty on the planting,' really holds true when it comes to a tree. If your tree is bare-rooted make sure that the roots don't dry out. Keep them covered with wet sacking.

1 Make a hole twice as big as the rootball, and get rid of all weeds.

2 Check the tree to see if it fits the hole. There should be room for the roots to spread out, with the graft just above the soil level.

3 Drive in a short stake off-centre. Backfill with some manure or compost mixed into the topsoil and add bonemeal for good measure.

4 Shake the tree as you plant it to get rid of air locks. Firm the soil down well and water copiously. Give the tree a pull to make sure it feels firm. Attach the tree to the stake with a tie, using a spacer.

5 During the first season, and until the tree gets its roots right down, water generously in dry weather.

# • PROJECT •
## MAKING A CORDON

Training trees so that they don't shade the next plot is a good idea for an allotment. Buy some two- or three-year-old fruit trees already shaped or some one-year-olds to train yourself. Look for those with side shoots and check the root stocks to make sure they will grow to an appropriate size. Autumn is the best time for planting, but winter will do. Trees on dwarf root stocks will need permanent staking. There are many shapes to choose from, but a cordon is the easiest.

**You will need**
- maiden trees
- stakes
- wires
- ties
- secateurs

1 Prepare the soil well.

2 Plant a one-year-old tree (maiden) and secure it to a cane at an angle of about 45 degrees, attaching it to the wires already fixed.

3 Do not prune the leader but cut back any side shoots (feathers) to four buds.

4 Remove any flowers in the first year, taking care not to damage the growing shoots just behind them.

5 In late summer cut back all mature side shoots to three leaves but leave the immature ones until autumn. Leave any that are less than 23 cm (9 in) as they usually have fruit buds on their tips.

6 Carry on until the tree reaches the desired height and trim off the leader.

If plants are given a flying start in life they will grow to be strong and resilient. Keep in mind their individual preferences and plant them in the right soil for their needs. Make sure they have enough light, air and water and that they are not competing with weeds.

# cultivation

5

## SOWING FROM SEED
Sowing seed outside
**PROJECT – *Making a seed bed***
Sowing seed indoors
Pricking out or potting on
Hardening off

## PROTECTING YOUR PLANTS
The cold greenhouse
The cold frame
Using cloches
Other protection methods

## MAINTAINING YOUR PLOT
Watering
Feeding
Organic feeds
Liquid feeds

◁ An abundant plot with rows of onions, cabbages, carrots and peas. Such a plot needs regular watering, feeding, and weeding.

# SOWING FROM
# seed

Tomatoes, aubergines, peppers and other vegetables that come from sunnier countries need a lot of sunshine to ripen. In cooler climes the summer can be too short so it is therefore often safer to buy a small plant. For the rest, though, there is nothing quite so exciting as growing vegetables from seed.

- SOWING SEED OUTSIDE
- **PROJECT ~** *Making a seed bed*
- SOWING SEED INDOORS
- PRICKING OUT OR POTTING ON
- HARDENING OFF

Choosing seeds is becoming easier as the selection of organic ones (those not treated with chemical fungicide) is growing every year; information about this should be found on the packet. When buying seeds, look for disease-resistant varieties and types that are less likely to bolt. F1 hybrids (a cross of two pure lines intended to bring out the best qualities of both parents) are expensive but reliable. However, they are driving out many old varieties, and you can get a fabulous selection of heritage seeds from seed libraries.

## SOWING SEED OUTSIDE

Many plants can be started off where they are intended to grow once the soil is warm enough.

Root vegetables do not take kindly to being transplanted. Generally hardy annuals and also lettuce, peas and spring onions are sown in their permanent positions. Get ahead by covering the area with clear plastic or cloches for about two weeks to warm the soil.

△ Large seeds, such as these Sugar Snap pea seeds, can be placed individually in rows, spacing them out to the correct distance.

◁ Smaller seeds should be scattered thinly in the seed drill. When the seedlings emerge, thin them out to leave just the strongest plants at the correct spacing.

# • PROJECT •

## MAKING A SEED BED

A seed bed saves work as only one small area needs to be kept in tip-top condition. It is useful for bringing on young plants, particularly those that have a long growing season and don't need much space to start with. While they are in the seed bed, you can use the land for faster crops. Leeks and brassicas are often started in a seed bed and transplanted later.

### You will need

- a rake
- short stakes
- twine
- a hoe
- seeds
- a watering can with a fine rose
- plant labels

**1** Before sowing, prepare the bed, making a fine tilth so that seedlings can push up through the ground effortlessly. If the soil is heavy, break it down with the back of a rake, then turn the rake over and go to and fro over the soil until you have an even surface with no lumps or stones.

**2** Stretch twine between short stakes and, using it as a guideline, make a shallow drill or trench with the corner of a hoe. If the soil is dry, dribble water along the trench.

**3** Carefully sprinkle fine seeds as thinly as possible along the trench by taking little pinches between finger and thumb. Don't plant them any deeper than recommended on the packet – doing so is the main reason for failure. If the seeds are large, place them individually in the drill.

**4** Cover the seeds with soil and firm it down with the back of a rake. If you have clay soil which is likely to form a crust or 'cap', use a proprietary compost to cover the seeds. If they grow too closely together, thin them down to the strongest. When watering them, use a fine rose on the can.

Transplant the seedlings in cool weather or in the evening, taking as much soil as you can with the plant to avoid damaging the roots. Plant them in generous holes, fill up with soil, firm it and water carefully. Plant brassicas slightly deeper than they were before in the seed bed.

### SOWING SEED INDOORS

Whether on a window-sill or in a greenhouse, sowing indoors has advantages. You can get ahead of the game by planting early when it is too cold to sow outside, and with the use of a propagator, you can grow tender crops including

▷ Protect young plants from pests and weather damage with glass or plastic cloches.

△ As the seedlings emerge, thin out the plants to leave space for them to develop. Remove all but the strongest seedlings, spaced in their final growing positions.

▷ When potting on seedlings, take care not to touch the delicate stalks. Handle the plants by their seed leaves (the largest, outer leaves) and firm the compost gently back around their roots slightly deeper than they were growing in the seed tray.

tomatoes, melons, peppers and aubergines – plants which might not otherwise have time to ripen in the short summers of cooler countries.

**1** Put some compost into the container and firm it down. You can grow seeds in any container. A foil tray, a yoghurt pot or a cut-off plastic bottle will be fine as long as there are drainage holes. Polystyrene blocks keep the seeds warm and give them a head start.

**2** Sow the seed sparsely. Sieve compost to cover the seeds or put in a layer of vermiculite or perlite (lightweight minerals which retain moisture but drain quickly) following packet directions.

**3** Stand the container in water and let the compost soak it up. Don't water the container from the top as you might wash away the seeds!

**4** Wrap the container in clingfilm, cover it with glass, or put it into a propagator. The seeds shouldn't need watering again until they have germinated. As soon as you see signs of life, remove the cover. Put the container in a light place out of direct sunlight. Keep some water at room temperature for watering but don't overdo it as the seedlings might 'damp off'. If they are on a window-sill, turn them every day, or put them in a box lined with kitchen foil to reflect light.

---

### GARDENER'S TIP

*Hygiene is vital when sowing seeds. Always use fresh compost to avoid disease and make sure that all tools and containers are scrubbed clean.*

---

## PRICKING OUT OR POTTING ON

This is not a job to be hurried. When the seedlings are big enough to handle they are ready to go. Water them ahead of time and have some containers filled with compost with a hole made with a dibber (or a pencil) to receive each plant. Ease out the seedlings with the dibber and, taking care not to touch the stems but just the leaves, move them to the new pots, with the first set of leaves just above the surface of the compost. Firm down the compost and water it carefully without soaking the seedlings.

## HARDENING OFF

Prepare the young plants for the world outside in stages. Wait till the weather is fair before putting them out under cloches or into the cold frame. Leave the lid of the frame off during the day and cover the plants at night. If the nights turn cold bring them back inside for a while. Avoid any extreme of temperature and keep them moist but not too wet. When they are ready to go into the ground, water them well before removing them from the pots. When they are planted, water them again to get rid of air pockets round the roots.

△ A well-stocked greenhouse with geraniums and vegetable seedlings in trays, ready for potting on.

# PROTECTING your plants

A greenhouse, cold frames, cloches and the use of plastic and fleece will extend the season and help you to get ahead. Much can be improvised by recycling old materials, including windows and plastic water bottles.

---

- THE COLD GREENHOUSE

- THE COLD FRAME

- USING CLOCHES

- OTHER PROTECTION METHODS
  Plastic bottles
  Polytunnels
  Horticultural fleece
  Plastic sheeting

---

## THE COLD GREENHOUSE

A cold greenhouse with a propagator at home (or an airing cupboard) can serve well for most allotment holders, as they generally concentrate their growing in the warmer months.

A cold greenhouse is useful for extending the season at both ends and for raising hardy plants for transplanting outside. Under glass they are protected from the elements and should get a smoother start. Providing the ideal environment in a greenhouse can be tricky.

• Greenhouses often become scorching in the day and icy at night and it's a question of juggling with the ventilation, watering and shading, and 'damping down' – wetting the staging and floor and spraying the plants with fine mist.

• Air-flow is important to avoid a build-up of pests and diseases, so leave the door and vents open as much as the weather allows.

• Be careful not to overwater the plants and don't splash the leaves, which can spread any lurking fungal disease.

• At the end of the season, the greenhouse needs a good scrub for the same reason.

• If cold weather threatens and you want a little more time, you can insulate it with bubble wrap for extra protection.

## THE COLD FRAME

A cold frame is invaluable for hardening off plants and growing tender ones. They are not difficult to make. The best types have wooden or brick sides

△ To keep a greenhouse at the right temperature takes some juggling with ventilation, watering and shading.

and a glass top which can be lifted off in the heat of the day and put back at night. Old window frames are perfect for this purpose. If chill weather descends you can add extra protection in the form of an old blanket or 'duvets' of newspaper balls in black bin-liners. Protection for tender crops like melons and aubergines can be improvised with upright sheets of glass on the sunny side of the plants or sheets of glass balanced against each other to make a pointed roof over delicate plants.

## USING CLOCHES

Cloches are immensely useful for warming the soil for about two weeks before planting, protecting young plants from sudden drops in

△ A handsome set of cold frames conveniently placed by the greenhouse. Seedlings and young plants can be brought out of the greenhouse for hardening off.

◁ A simple tunnel made from polythene stretched over a series of wire hoops. The sides of the polythene can be lifted on warm days.

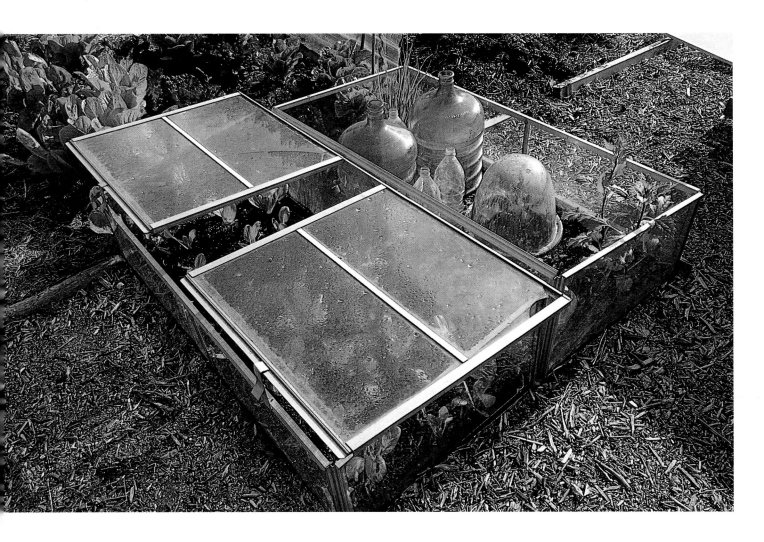

△ Moving the glass on and off the cold frame allows you to adjust the temperature and keep it as even as possible.

▷ Ornamental cloches are available to buy but a plastic water bottle with the bottom cut off and cap removed is just as effective.

temperature, winds and pests. They can extend the season of half-hardy plants and protect overwintering crops. Before removing them acclimatize the plant by increasing the ventilation slowly over a couple of weeks to harden it off in stages. Be watchful as cloche protection can provide the ideal warm, damp conditions for the rapid spread of fungal diseases or reflect fierce light causing leaf scorch.

## OTHER PROTECTION METHODS

• **Horticultural fleece**, which is made from polypropylene, has been a real breakthrough. As light as flotsam, it doesn't weigh down plants and it lets in light, air and water as well as excluding pests. Whole crops can be grown under screens of it until they mature. It is also useful as a winter wrapping around more tender plants to keep

them warm in winter. Cut to the desired size with scissors, leaving a generous border which you can secure with pegs, soil or stones. The covering needs to be fixed tightly enough not to flap. Let the edges out as the plants grow.

• **Plastic bottles** with the bottoms cut off and the caps open for air to flow, make excellent cloches for small plants.

• **Plastic sheeting** can be used in the same way as fleece. You need to make plenty of holes or slits in it for ventilation and it needs to be watched carefully as harmful humidity can build up fast. It is good for warming the soil two weeks before planting. Use transparent sheeting only.

• **Polytunnels** are useful for covering larger areas and are easily made, large or small, with polythene or horticultural fleece stretched over a framework of wire hoops.

△ Horticultural fleece is used here to protect cabbage seedlings from pests, though it also offers good protection against cold weather.

◁ A small polytunnel can easily be made by covering wire hoops with fleece or polythene. Bury the ends of the polythene or fleece in the soil to hold them tightly in place.

# MAINTAINING
# your plot

**Most of the spadework on the allotment is done from spring onwards and by mid-summer, maintenance is the key.**

- WATERING

- FEEDING
  - Nitrogen
  - Phosphorus
  - Potassium
  - Magnesium
  - Iron
  - Calcium, manganese and sulphur

- ORGANIC FEEDS
  - Bone meal
  - Blood, fish and bone
  - Dried blood
  - Dried manures
  - Fish meal
  - Hoof and horn
  - Rock potash
  - Seaweed meal
  - Wood ash

- LIQUID FEEDS
  - Seaweed extract
  - Comfrey
  - Nettles

Once the allotment is planted out for the season, the main tasks are watering, weeding, feeding, deadheading, staking, tying in climbers, summer pruning, harvesting, and pest and disease control. A little effort day by day is more productive than an occasional blitz.

## WATERING

If you can, water in the cool of evening to avoid evaporation. It is better to water generously less often than to sprinkle frequently. The aim is to get the roots to go deep. Superficial watering encourages plants to grow roots near the surface which dry out quickly. With thirsty plants like courgettes or tomatoes, sink a piece of pipe alongside them and pour water down it to get right to the roots. When planting, really soak the soil (or wait for a good rainfall) and then apply a thick mulch (not quite touching the plant) to conserve moisture. However, take care not to overwater plants when they are being propagated or when in a greenhouse, as this can lead to disease.

## FEEDING

If you have high soil fertility you shouldn't need to feed much, but occasionally you might want to give your crops a boost. This applies particularly to hungry ones like tomatoes or those that have overwintered. The exact amount and the type of feed depends on the plants and whether you want to improve the fruit and flowers or put on leaf growth. The major elements for plant growth

△ A small allotment with a harvest of beans, onoins and potatoes. A long-handled hoe is used to weed between the plants to avoid treading on the soil and compacting it.

**GARDENER'S TIP**

*Hopefully, you will have got rid of the worst of the weeds when you took over the plot though it can take a few seasons to eliminate them completely. Mulching is the best line of defence against weeds but chase up annual weeds with hand or hoe. Catch them young so that they don't compete with your plants for nutrients, light and water.*

*Leave a selected few in odd corners – nettles, black medick, dandelion and red campion for butterflies; wild poppies, chickweed, teasel for birds; groundsel and toadflax for bees and butterflies, and fat hen for hoverflies.*

◁ Leave wild flowers in corners for friendly insects and grow a few daisy-type flowers such as chrysanthemums, sunflowers or marigolds to encourage them.

are nitrogen, phosphorus and potassium (potash), labelled as NPK. Plants also need calcium, sulphur and magnesium, and trace elements including manganese and iron. They get the other essentials – oxygen, carbon and hydrogen – from the air, sunlight and water.

▽ Watering is essential, especially in the warm, summer months. Water in the cool of evening to prevent evaporation and scorching.

• **Nitrogen** encourages leaf growth and gives plants their greenness. Too little and the plants will be stunted and the leaves pale. Too much will produce sappy growth which will attract pests and collapse at the first sign of frost.

• **Phosphorus** encourages healthy growth throughout the plant, especially the roots. Only small quantities are needed. A lack of it will show as stunted growth and a purple or red discoloration appearing first on the older leaves.

• **Potassium** is associated with the size and quality of flowers and fruit. A lack of it will show up as small fruit and flowers and yellowing or browning of the leaves.

• **Magnesium** forms chlorophyll, the greening constituent. A lack is usually a sign of insufficient organic matter in the soil. Magnesium deficiency causes chlorosis, the symptom of which is yellowing of the leaves, starting between the veins.

• **Iron** plays much the same role as magnesium, though it's only needed in tiny quantities. A deficiency is more common on alkaline soils.

• **Calcium, manganese and sulphur** are generally in plentiful supply in soil when rotted organic matter has been added.

▷ Russian comfrey makes great liquid fertilizer but it has an unpleasant smell when it rots down.

## ORGANIC FEEDS

• **Bone meal** is high in phosphate for root growth and is helpful when planting shrubs and trees.

• **Blood, fish and bone** meal is a balanced NPK fertilizer.

• **Dried blood** is high in nitrogen and is used as a quick tonic.

• **Dried manures** have all the trace elements but are low in NPK.

• **Fish meal** contains nitrogen and phosphate.

• **Hoof and horn** is high in nitrogen and works on a slow release. It needs time to break down, so apply to the soil a week or so before planting.

• **Rock potash** is a useful source of potash.

• **Seaweed meal** is a slow-release all-round tonic with all the trace elements.

• **Wood ash** is high in potassium and has some phosphate, though quantities of each depend on the type of timber burned.

## LIQUID FERTILIZERS

• **Seaweed extract** is a good tonic supplying the full range of trace elements. However, it is easy to make your own fertilizers out of comfrey, nettles, or sheep, cow, horse or goat manure. The technique is to tie it up in a sack and leave it to soak in water over a matter of weeks.

• **Comfrey** is a superb all-round fertilizer. The leaves can be used as an activator on the compost heap, thrown down into a potato trench or laid as mulch around crops – though as it is alkaline it is not advisable to use it on chalky soils. Its long roots draw up potassium from the subsoil. It is almost impossible to get rid of as the roots are so deep. Site it where it can stay for twenty years or more or persuade your committee to plant a patch of it. The recommended type is Russian comfrey *(Symphytum x uplandicum Blocking 14)* which, unlike other types, will not spread. As Russian comfrey rarely sets seed, the best way to start it off is to beg or buy some root

offsets. Plant them in spring or early autumn, though any time will do except deepest winter when they are dormant. Incorporate some well-rotted compost into the soil, clear any weeds and then plant the offsets 60 to 90 cm (2 to 3 ft) apart, with their growing points just below the surface.

Don't harvest them in the first year but remove the flowering stems, and go easy in the second year while the plants build up strength. After this, comfrey can be cut back three or four times a year with shears when the leaves are about 60 cm (2 ft) high.

Don't let it flower as this will weaken the plant. A concentrate can be made by letting the leaves rot in a container with a hole in the base and a vessel underneath it. Dilute the concentrate with water in the ratio of about 15:1. The only disadvantage of comfrey is the smell it gives off as it rots down.

• **Nettles** make a good general tonic though with less phosphate. Like comfrey, they are not suitable for alkaline soils. Nettles gathered in spring are the richest in nutrients.

△ Allotments in Madeira, where the terracing prevents soil erosion in wet weather and helps with irrigation.

◁ The humble stinging nettle attracts wildlife and can be made into a highly nutritious liquid fertilizer.

There has to be a bit of give and take in an organic allotment – you need a few bugs around to feed the predators. Aim for a happy balance. If you have a good cross-section of robust plants and encourage wildlife, you already hold the winning cards.

# the rogues'
## gallery

6

**KNOW THE ENEMY**
Friend or foe?
Pests
Diseases
Useful predators

**PEST AND DISEASE CONTROL**
Barriers
Traps
Companion planting

**ORGANIC PESTICIDES AND FUNGICIDES**
A-Z directory
Golden rules for spraying

**COMMON PESTS AND DISEASES**
A-Z directory

◁ Flowers such as Californian poppies and marigolds are useful for drawing in friendly insects which will eat unwanted pests.

# KNOW THE
# enemy

Get one step ahead of pests with netting, trapping and timing, and combining plants in such a way as to put them off the scent. Grow plants fast to minimize the opportunities for pests to thrive. Be observant and nip problems in the bud.

- FRIEND OR FOE?
- PESTS
- DISEASES
- USEFUL PREDATORS

## FRIEND OR FOE?

Learn to distinguish friend from foe. Generally creatures that move fast are chasing prey and the slow ones are after your vegetables – but not always! A ladybird larva, for example, could easily be mistaken for an enemy. Some creatures are pests at one stage of their lives and predators at another. For example, wasps keep down pests but can also wreck your fruit.

## PESTS

Some pests are large enough to be seen; many are not or else they dine at night. Detection skills come in here, finding clues from the type of damage.

- If there are holes in the leaves, the chances are they are being eaten by slugs, snails or caterpillars.
- If it's the roots, it may be underground larvae.
- If the leaves are curling, it is most likely aphids feeding on plant sap on the undersides.
- If you find your vegetables decapitated one morning, it could be the work of cutworms.
- If some newly planted seedlings disappear without trace, suspect mice.

## DISEASES

Diseases are caused by fungi, viruses, and bacteria. Symptoms include spotting where parts of leaves die, cankers or scabs, changing colour (yellowing or silvering), wilting, wet rots and powdery or fluffy moulds or mildew. Viruses are bad news, as there is no cure for them. The symptoms are malformations and unnatural patterns on

△ Turnips need very fine mesh netting to protect them from attacks by tiny flea beetles.

◁ Lacewings (which can be green, brown or black) and their larvae will demolish aphid colonies.

▽ Ladybirds, from the larval stage onwards, get through thousands of aphids and other small insects in their lifetimes.

**USEFUL PREDATORS**

- Ladybirds, hoverflies and lacewings demolish aphids, mites, scale insects, mealy bugs and small caterpillars at an astonishing rate.
- Ground beetles eat slugs, underground larvae and root aphids.
- Parasitic wasps eat caterpillars.
- Centipedes eat slugs and snails.
- Earwigs eat caterpillars, aphids and codling moth eggs.
- Frogs, toads, hedgehogs, newts and slow-worms demolish slugs and many other pests.
- Birds eat a wide range of pests, as do bats.

leaves (mottling or mosaic). They start on a single plant and spread by anything that moves from plant to plant – including you. When accepting gifts of plants, be careful of disease. If in doubt, isolate the plants for a while.

Buy disease-resistant varieties or certified virus-free stock when possible. As soon as you find diseased material, remove it and, taking care not to shake the spores around, either burn it or put it in a bin-liner, get it off the site and wash your hands. Tools and pots should be cleaned, and sterilized with alcohol, to avoid cross-infection.

◁ A small 'moat' made from old guttering, kept topped up with water, makes an effective barrier against slugs and snails.

# PEST AND DISEASE
# control

**Armed with a little knowledge of which pests are likely to attack which plants, their lifestyles, breeding habits, size, method of attack and so on, it is quite easy to outwit them by simple means.**

- BARRIERS
    Cloches
    Collars
    Grease bands
    Nets

- TRAPS
    Grease traps
    Pheromone traps
    Sticky grease bands

- COMPANION PLANTING

Pests can be deterred by barriers, caught in traps, confused by scent or, as the last resort, destroyed with organic sprays. These are less persistent than their synthetic counterparts which mean they are less likely to find their way into the food chain or waterways, causing less damage to the ecology. None the less, they should be avoided if at all possible.

## BARRIERS

- **Cloches** will keep out slugs as well as flying insects and birds.
- **Collars** of carpet underlay around plants will deter root flies and soil-borne creatures, many of which lay their eggs under the plant so that their larvae have food around them as they grow.
- **Grease bands** around trees and shrubs will deter climbing pests. Many types are available.

◁ A collar to deter slugs, cabbage root fly and other soil-borne pests can be made from foam-backed carpet or underlay and placed around the plant stem.

△ Surrounding carrots with a low barrier of fleece effectively protects them from carrot fly as the flies fly close to the ground.

• **Nets** These need to go up before the pests arrive and the gauge of wire mesh used needs to be in proportion to the pest. For the smallest pests use horticultural fleece.

## TRAPS

• **Grease traps** Car-grease spread on a board will trap some insects when the plant is shaken.

• **Pheromone traps** use a synthetic hormone to attract and trap various moths.

• **Sticky grease bands**, commercially bought, are effective against moths which attack apples, pears and plums. Jars of diluted beer sunk in the ground will send slugs off into drunken oblivion.

## COMPANION PLANTING

French marigolds *(Calendula)* or nasturtiums *(Tropaeolum)* mask the smell of brassicas to the cabbage white butterfly, and if four rows of onions are planted around one row of carrots,

◁ Humming nylon tape will scare birds. Old CDs on a line work as well – they flash as they catch the light.

they keep carrot fly at bay until the onion leaves go over. Trials of dwarf, broad or French beans planted between brassicas of the same size in alternate rows show a lessening in aphid attack. The outer row must be beans. However, these pests are effectively deterred by barriers.

▽ Echium among courgettes attracts friendly predators and pollinating insects.

# **ORGANIC** pesticides and fungicides

Organic chemicals should be used with as much care as their synthetic counterparts and only as a last resort. Make sure that you have identified the problem accurately and target it precisely. The main advantage of organic chemicals over inorganic ones is that they are not persistent – in most cases they are active for no longer than a day. Don't attempt to make your own pesticides. It is illegal to do so in the UK.

**BACILLUS THURINGIENSIS** (known as Bt) is the name of a caterpillar disease. Bt contains spores and protein crystals which can be sprayed on brassicas and other plants to protect them from moth and other caterpillars. **Warning:** it will kill a wide range of caterpillars as well as those which are pests.

**COPPER FUNGICIDE** is highly effective against fungal diseases, coating the leaves for several weeks. It comes in various cocktails including Bordeaux mixture, which is copper sulphate and slaked lime, and Burgundy mixture, which is copper sulphate mixed with washing soda. **Warning:** it is toxic to fish and can harm plants, particularly those under stress.

**DERRIS** (rotenone) comes as a powder or liquid and is made from the roots of derris plants. It is an effective insecticide for aphids, spider mites and other small insects but is also poisonous to ladybirds and worms. **Warning:** wear gloves and protective clothing when using.

**INSECTICIDAL SOAP** is potassium salt soap and is used to control aphids, whitefly, red spider mites and mealy bugs. It works only if it scores a direct hit and is active for only a day. **Warning:** friendly insects will be killed if they are in contact with the spray.

**PYRETHRUM** is extracted from *Chrysanthemum* coccineum and is used as an insecticide against aphids, small caterpillars and flea beetle, among others. **Warning:** it is poisonous to fish and some friendly insects.

△ If you do need to use a spray, choose a windless evening and target precisely.

▷ The strong smell of onions will confuse and deter some pests, such as carrot fly.

**SOFT SOAP** is a mild pesticide but is usually used as a medium or wetter to help other sprays adhere to leaves.

**Sulphur** is another fungicide which comes as a spray or dust and can be used to control mildew. **Warning:** it is harmful to beneficial insects.

---

**GOLDEN RULES FOR SPRAYING**
- Follow the manufacturer's instructions to the letter.
- Store the sprays away from children in the original labelled containers.
- Wash equipment thoroughly afterwards, having disposed of any leftovers.
- Never spray open flowers for fear of harming bees.
- Spray only on windless evenings when the good insects will have turned in for the night.

# COMMON pests and diseases

**APHIDS** There are hundreds of different types of this very common pest which include greenfly and blackfly, mealy cabbage aphids and lettuce root aphids. They breed like crazy, suck the sap of plants and secrete honeydew which brings on sooty moulds (a harmless fungus) and they spread viruses as they move from plant to plant.
• Encourage hoverflies, lacewings and ladybirds (see chapter 3, p. 36 and chapter 5, p. 77). They will vacuum them up.
• Choose resistant varieties.
• In the case of broad beans, beat the black bean aphid season by planting early under cover. If you do get caught, cut off the tops of the plants where the insects congregate.
• Cover with horticultural fleece, though not if plants still need to be pollinated.
• Squash the insects or cut off infected shoots and drop them into soapy water.
• Wash the aphids off with a powerful jet of water.
• Spray the plants with soft soap or insecticide soap.

**ASPARAGUS BEETLES** are chequered black and yellow. They will defoliate asparagus and stay in the soil over the winter.
• Clear up all debris.
• Use derris liquid or dust.

**BIRDS** When soft fruit is ripening birds can strip it with the speed of light. Pigeons are partial to young brassicas and can decimate a crop.

• Use netting and bird scarers. Anything that flaps in the wind will help. Old CDs tied along lines are effective as they swirl and flash as the light catches them.

**BLACKCURRANT GALL MITES** (big bud) breed inside the flower buds, making them swell.
• Buy good stock.
• Remove and burn all affected buds.
• If the infestation is very bad you can cut the bush to ground level and start afresh the following year.

**BOTRYTIS** see grey mould.

**CABBAGE BUTTERFLY** The caterpillars of the large white type are hairy and yellow with black markings. They feed on outer leaves of brassicas.
• Pick the affected leaves off. The larvae of the small white cabbage butterfly are green and velvety and eat cabbage hearts. Catch them before they burrow in.

**CABBAGE MOTH** caterpillars eat the leaves of cabbages and cauliflowers. They vary in colour from green to light brown. Pick them off and use netting, *Bacillus thuringiensis*, pyrethrum or derris spray or dust.

**CABBAGE ROOT FLIES** bore into the roots of all brassicas and overwinter in the soil.
• Put collars of carpet around the plants and cover the plants with fleece.
• Dig the ground over in winter so that the birds will eat the maggots.

**CANKERS** are caused by fungi and bacteria which make malformations in the roots and stems of woody plants, particularly fruit trees.
• Remove diseased parts, cutting back to healthy tissue, and burn them.
• Improve growing conditions.
**Parsnip canker** shows itself as red marks on the tops of the roots and sets off rotting.
• Throw the plants away and buy resistant varieties.

**CARROT FLIES** tunnel unseen into carrots, celeriac, parsnips, parsley and celery. They fly low, so vertical barriers of fleece will frustrate them effectively.

**CELERY FLIES** are little maggots which eat the leaves.
• Catch them early and pick off and burn the affected leaves.

△ Cabbage butterfly caterpillar.

**CELERY LEAF SPOT** is caused by fungus and spreads rapidly in damp conditions.
• Destroy and burn plants.
• Use resistant seed in a rotation system.
• Treat plants with copper fungicide.

**CHOCOLATE SPOT** is a fungal disease, affecting broad beans in particular. Small brown spots appear on the leaves, especially in wet weather.
• Make sure that broad beans have good rich soil, air circul-ation and sharp drainage.
• Pull out any that are badly damaged.
• Clear weeds and debris.
• Treat plants with copper fungicide.

**CLUB ROOT** is a bad and widespread disease of the cabbage family (which includes broccoli, Brussels sprouts, kale, kohlrabi, swedes and turnips). It can live in the soil for twenty years and is almost impossible to destroy. The first signs are sick-looking plants. The roots become distorted, forming a 'club' (like an elbow) or a series of tuber-like swellings. Club root thrives in acid, wet soil and is easily spread by tools, footwear or composts.
• Provide the best growing conditions with lots of fertility and good drainage.
• If your soil is acid, add lime well in advance of planting the crop – a year ahead if possible.
• Rotation is vital. If club root has set in, avoid the same piece of soil for brassi-cas for as many years as you can.
• Don't use mustard as a green manure as it is also prone to the disease.
• Give plants a better chance by grow-ing them in sterile compost in pots

before transplanting. Remove all infected plants and destroy them.
• Be very careful not to spread the dis-ease on tools and shoes.
• Buy resistant varieties to avoid trouble.

**CORAL SPOT** is an orange-coloured fungus that will get into a wound or a dead branch and causes die-back. Currants are particularly vulnerable.
• Prune out all affected stems down to healthy wood and burn the cuttings.

**CUTWORMS**, which can sever the stem entirely on a wide range of fruit and vegetables, are the larvae of a group of moths. They lay thousands of eggs around the stems of plants in summer. The caterpillars, which are in varying shades of brown, yellow and green, feed first on the leaves and then drop down to do worse damage. You will find them under the soil surface.
• Clear weeds, in which moths lay eggs.
• Put a collar of carpet underlay around the stems.
• Turn over the soil for the birds to find the eggs in winter.

**FLEA BEETLES** jump. Small and shiny, they emerge in spring and can fly long distances to find food. Young brassicas are their favourite fare and they leave holes in leaves and stems.
• Prevent their attacks by covering young plants with cloches or fleece.
• If you get an infestation, put boards smeared with car-grease or slow-drying glue under the plants and shake them. The beetles will leap into the trap.
• Clear debris round plants.
• Use derris powder.

**GREY MOULD** or **BOTRYTIS** is a common disease, particularly during damp summers, causing buds, leaves and flowers to rot. It's a fluffy mould which, when disturbed, releases clouds of spores, infecting all around it.
• Avoid overcrowding, clear any rotting vegetation around plants as this will harbour the mould, and improve air-flow.
• Remove all diseased plants as soon as possible.

**HALO BLIGHT** is a bacterial disease producing spots in the centre of a pale 'halo' in beans and other pod vegeta-bles. The disease comes in the seeds.
• Start again with seed from a fresh source.

**LEAF SPOT** is a fungal, seed-borne disease which affects a wide range of plants, including peas and broad beans, covering the leaves with brown spots with a lighter centre. The spots don't usually do too much damage. They can also be caused by bacteria.
• Pick off and burn affected leaves.
• Don't water from above or handle the plants when they are wet.
• Treat plants with copper fungicide.

**LEAF MOULD** is a disease usually confined to indoor tomatoes in high humidity. A greenish fungal growth on the undersides of leaves causes yellow patches on the upper sides and leaves shrivel and die. It is very infectious.
• Choose resistant varieties.
• Destroy diseased material. Keep the greenhouse well ventilated.
• Don't water from above.
• Treat plants with copper fungicide.

**LEAF SPOT** is a general term for a group of fungal diseases that cause spotting – black spot is a common one. The spots are dead areas and as they spread leaves drop off.
• Remove and burn affected leaves.
• Make sure the plants have plenty of air circulating around them.
• Treat plants with copper fungicide.

**MICE** sometimes steal newly planted seedlings and raid your shed.
• Use cloches to protect plants or traps to catch the mice.

**MILDEW** is a fungal disease which comes in various forms. It thrives in close damp conditions.
• Keep plants well ventilated, remove debris and burn any infected leaves.
• Treat plants with copper fungicide.
**Downy mildew** can be detected by the yellow patches on leaves with corresponding flufffy grey to purplish spots underneath. They will turn brown, sometimes become distorted, and die. It is fairly common on lettuce, spinach, onions and peas.
**Powdery mildew** is less damaging as it stays on the outside of the plant. It is grey and covers all parts.

**ONION FLY** is a small grey fly, the white maggots of which eat the roots of young onions and occasionally leeks, garlic and shallots. You can detect their presence by the yellowing of the outer leaves and you can spot them if you hoe around the roots. The second generation sometimes bores into the roots.
• Destroy the plants before the maggots return to the soil to pupate.

• If you grow from onion sets rather than seed, you will not need to thin them and will therefore avoid releasing the smell that attracts the flies.

**PEA** and **BEAN WEEVILS** can be detected by the U-shaped holes in the leaves of peas and broad beans. Tiny greyish beetles, they do not usually put plants at risk except seedlings.
• Use cloches to protect the plants
• Use a sprinkling of derris powder if the attack is severe.

**PEA MOTHS** are tiny caterpillars with black heads. They lay their eggs on the flowers to hatch out inside the pea pod.
• Avoid them by planting early or late to avoid the breeding time.
• Cover the peas with fine mesh when they are in flower.
• Turn over the soil for the birds to get at the moths in winter.
• Use derris liquid a week after flowering and again two weeks later.

**POTATO BLIGHT** see tomato and potato blight.

**POTATO SCAB** is a fungus disease, usually occurring in wet weather on heavy soils. Circular scabby patches appear on the tubers, which can burst, releasing spores.
• Destroy the crop and start again with fresh soil. Consider using raised beds.

**RED SPIDER MITES** are spider-like creatures which develop colonies on leaves, sucking the sap of many different plants. Invisible to the naked eye, their presence is revealed as leaves

take on a mottled yellowing.
• They like dry conditions best, so a good spray of water on a regular basis will help to keep them at bay.
• Use derris liquid at three six-day intervals.

**RASPBERRY BEETLES** feed on the blossoms and the larvae burrow into the fruits.
• Expose the ground around the canes so birds find the overwintering pupae.
• Use derris to treat the plants.

**SLUGS** are a universal menace. There are many different species, from the small dark grey European garden slug to the great slug or the spotted garden slug, which is familiar to American gardeners. Some live underground and attack roots and tubers; others attack below and above ground, and there is even one (a species of *Testacella*, which has a little shell at the back) which is carnivorous and eats earthworms and other slugs. Slugs like warm moist weather and come out to feed at night. They shelter and breed under stones, in piles of leaves, under garden debris, in the soil – and under mulch (the one disadvantage of using it).

△ Grey field slug.

• Encourage predators including frogs, toads, birds, hedgehogs, shrews and beetles. You can bring in frogs and toads by creating a small pond.

• Cover small plants with cloches.

• Surround them with inhospitable sharp mulches – gravel and eggshells – or dry ones – wood chips, soot, ash, lime.

•Hold torchlight vigils and catch and destroy the slugs by dropping them into a strong salt solution or paraffin. Using tongs or rubber gloves makes this slightly less repellent.

• Trap and drown them by sinking plastic pots of diluted beer or milk into the ground, changing the bait from time to time and stopping if you catch beetles.

• Scooped-out melon and grapefruit skins make hiding places for them to congregate, as do old planks or wet newspaper.

• Lay out alternative food sources. They will choose rotting vegetation over fresh, so old lettuce leaves kept moist under cover of a tile will draw them away to where they can be collected.

• There are effective predators (parasitic nematodes) which can be bought and watered on, but they are expensive and last for only six weeks, so are unsuited to large allotments.

**SNAILS** present the same problems as slugs and the same treatments are effective, though frogs won't eat them.

**SOFT ROT** is a bacterial and fungal disease which results in the decay of plant tissues. It affects swedes and turnips, showing as a greyish mushy rot on heavy wet ground.

• Try raised beds for better drainage.

**TOMATO** and **POTATO BLIGHT** shows as brown marks on leaves and stems and a white mass of fungal spores on the undersides. The tomato fruits and potato tubers develop sunken areas and tomatoes can get leathery patches. Other fungi and bacteria join in to induce a fast-spreading, highly infectious soft rot. The spores can blow in from miles away.

• Buy resistant strains and good quality seed potatoes. Early varieties are more prone to this blight than main-crop ones.

• Remove and destroy infected leaves.

• Space plants widely for air circulation, and water them at ground level.

• Earth up and mulch potatoes with straw to prevent spores reaching tubers.

• Dig up all tubers at the end of the season.

• Treat plants with copper fungicide.

**VIOLET ROOT ROT** shows up as violet fungal threads covering the roots, crowns and stems of plants. It can affect asparagus, beetroot, carrots, celery, parsnips, potatoes, strawberries, swedes and turnips. The first signs are yellowing and stunting. It's most commonly found in wet acid soils.

• Remove and destroy the crop.

• Change the conditions and try again.

△ Garden snail.

**VIRUSES** come in many forms, all incurable. The first signs are loss of vigour and stunting, followed by strange colour changes and patterns on leaves, including mosaic patterns and mottling.

• Viruses are mostly spread by aphids, so the first step is to control them.

**Cucumber mosaic virus** does not just attack cucumbers – it can affect a wide range of plants including marrows, courgettes, peppers and spinach. The leaves will develop unnatural yellow patterns and the fruits will be distorted.

• Burn affected plants, taking great care not to spread the infection.

• Buy resistant varieties.

• Remove weeds and debris in which the spores may overwinter.

**WHITEFLIES** are tiny flying insects which suck the sap on the underside of leaves and excrete copious amounts of sticky honeydew.

• Shake the plants and suck them up with a portable vacuum cleane.

• Spray them with insecticidal soap.

**WIREWORMS** are orange click-beetle larvae that live underground and bore holes into carrots and potatoes. They are mostly found in grassland and the good news is that, as your allotment becomes more thoroughly cultivated with less grass, they will diminish.

• You can trap them by planting some wheat or burying carrots, a cabbage or a potato on a stick to attract them away from your crops. The bait can then be dug up and destroyed.

• Keep the ground free of weeds.

• If you dig over the soil in winter the birds will find the larvae and eat them.

As summer draws to a close, think about increasing your stock for next year. Artichokes and rhubarb can be divided and soft fruit layered to make new plants. Collecting and storing seed is good organic practice as it rarely carries disease.

# the harvest

7

**PLANT PROPAGATION**

◁ When autumn approaches it is time to harvest all the fruits of your labour, such as these pumpkins in an allotment in Vermont in the US.

# PLANT
## propagation

**Most gardeners would agree that they get their greatest kick from seeing their plants shoot up as if by magic from seed, and increasing stock from cuttings or division is very satisfying.**

- SEEDS AND BULBS
  Peas and beans
  Shallots and garlic

- DIVISION
  Rhubarb
  Globe artichokes

- SOFTWOOD CUTTINGS

- TIP LAYERING

## SEEDS AND BULBS

Saving seed can become quite addictive. One disadvantage of having an allotment is that there is a lot of cross-pollination, so unless you isolate plants you could end up with some interesting varieties – cauliflower crossed with cabbage, for example!

- **Peas** and **beans** are self-pollinating and should come true to type. Leave some pods on the best specimens until they are brown and dry. If bad weather threatens, pull up the whole plant and hang it upside down in the shed. When the skins of the pods are crackly, shell them and reduce the moisture content further to prolong the life of the seed. Put them in the airing cupboard for a week or two. If they shatter when hit with a hammer they are ready. Store in paper bags and keep them cool and dry.

- **Shallots** and **garlic** make clusters of new bulbs. Dry them in a warm, shady, airy place for a couple of months and then cut off the tops about 2.5 cm (1 in) above the bulb. Separate the sections, remove the dry skins and store in mesh bags in a cool dry place. Old tights or stockings are also good for this purpose. Discard any damaged or sprouting bulbs.

## DIVISION

Many perennial plants can be divided.

**1** Cut back foliage and lift the entire plant and if it is muddy give it a wash.

**2** If it is a small clump you can divide it with a

△ The seeds of peas and beans should come true to type as they are self-pollinating.

knife, discarding the old centre and making sure there is a bud and some root on each piece. Large clumps can be split with a spade or, if they have a tangle of roots, plunge two forks into the clump back to back and lever it apart.

• **Rhubarb** should be split when the leaves have died down in autumn.

• **Globe artichokes** need to be divided every three years to stay in peak condition. The time to do this is in spring when they start to shoot. Drive a spade down, cutting off the offsets with a bit of root and shoot in each one.

## SOFTWOOD CUTTINGS

Cuttings from shrubs and herbaceous perennials should be made from a healthy shoot of this year's growth in late summer.

**1** Cut off a piece about 10 cm (4 in) long.

**2** Trim it on the slant with a sharp, clean knife just below a bud or leaf joint. Trim off the side leaves, leaving a couple on the top.

**3** Dip the bottom of the shoot into copper fungicide solution, plant it in a seed tray and water. A propagator helps, as heat from the bottom will encourage root growth.

## TIP LAYERING

This is an easy way to make more plants. It works particularly well with the briar fruits – blackberries and loganberries. In the summer, choose a good healthy stem that is still attached to the main plant and plant it tip down to a depth of about 15 cm (6 in). Within weeks it will shoot and root and you can sever it from the parent.

◁ To increase your stock of the briar fruits, bend over a healthy stem and plant it tip down. It will root and shoot within weeks.

◁ Marjoram, like many herbaceous perennials, can be lifted and split to make more plants. Replant the new sections and keep them well watered until they are established.

# STORING
# the harvest

Enjoy your harvest throughout the winter by freezing, storing, drying and bottling and by making jams, preserves and wine. Culinary herbs can be dried or frozen for flavouring and scented leaves and petals made into pot pourri.

- HOW TO STORE PRODUCE
  Potatoes
  Onions and garlic
  Beetroot, carrots, celeriac, kohlrabi, parsnips, swedes and turnips
  Apples
  Pears
  Herbs
- THE END OF THE SEASON
- AUTUMN TASKS
- THE WINTER ALLOTMENT

## HOW TO STORE PRODUCE

While most vegetables and soft fruit go into the freezer, the bulky vegetables can be stored dry. Take care not to break the skin or bruise crops when harvesting, as one rotten apple can ruin a whole barrel. Store only the best in a dry and airy place and check from time to time, removing anything suspicious. Early crops store less well than main crops.

- **Potatoes** are stored in the dark in thick paper (not plastic) sacks tied at the top. They should be kept above 5°C (37°F).
- **Onions** and **garlic** should be dried in the sun for a few days and then be made into strings or put into nets and hung in a cool airy spot.

- **Beetroot, carrots, celeriac, kohlrabi, parsnips, swedes** and **turnips** store well in a dry and airy place as long as they are undamaged. Twist off the leaves and pack them, unwashed, in wooden crates in layers with sand or sawdust in between.
- **Apples** should be picked on a dry day. Do this by cupping the fruit in one hand so as not to bruise them and gently twisting. Make sure you leave on some stalk. Wrap them individually in oiled or waxed paper and store in boxes or crates in a cool airy place.
- **Pears** are picked while still hard and stored in a single layer, unwrapped, with the stalks pointing upwards. Bring them indoors to ripen when you want them.

△ Hang complete stalks of Brussels sprouts in a cool, dry shed for storage. They will keep well for many weeks.

• **Herbs** for drying should be picked just before flowering on a dry day, tied in bunches and hung up in an airy spot. Once dry, the leaves can be crumbled and stored in jars. Herbs can also be used with scented petals to make pot pourri.

You can make your own sun-dried tomatoes, as well as dried apples, plums and pears. To dry fruit, cut it into rings and either dry them in the sun or in a very cool oven for several hours. Pack in layers between waxed paper.

▽ The autumn harvest often comes all at once though much can be made into soups and frozen to enjoy in the cold months ahead.

▷ After harvesting, onions need to dry out in the sun before they can be made into strings for hanging.

## THE END OF THE SEASON

• In autumn, fork the summer compost onto the beds for next year and make a new compost heap with the remains of the harvest along with weeds and prunings to rot down through the winter.

• Gather all the fallen leaves to add to it or to make leaf mould.

• Prune out the old fruiting canes of blackberries, raspberries and the briars.

• Check that stakes are secure and ties are not too tight.

• Disconnect the downpipes to the water-butts to avoid flooding.

• Plant spring cabbage, broad beans, garlic and ornamental bulbs.

• You may have sown an overwintering green manure in late summer to improve the soil and stop it leaching. If not, decide how to leave the ground. If there are weedy areas, put down old carpet or black plastic, or, if there's been a problem with soil-borne pests, turn over the ground for the birds to find them. If the soil is heavy clay, dig it over to allow frosts to break it down.

• Clean the greenhouse, wash out the flowerpots, discarding old compost. Clean and oil your tools.

▷ Turn over the soil in autumn to allow the frost to break down the heavy clods.

### AUTUMN TASKS

• Come autumn, cut down peas and beans, leaving their roots in the soil. If you have grown them on wire netting, burn off any remaining debris to get rid of disease.

• Dig out all the harvested brassica stumps and cut off the yellowing leaves of any you are leaving.

• Earth up sprouts, celery, celeriac and leeks to keep them stable in winter winds.

• Cut down the foliage of Jerusalem artichokes and asparagus and mulch them with manure or compost.

• Protect plants with cloches or fleece.

• Put fresh straw under the strawberry leaves.

• Dig up endives and store them in boxes of sand to make chicons through the winter.

• Bend the leaves over cauliflowers.

• Rake up leaves and compost them. Don't be too tidy. Leave some berries, seedheads and habitats for the birds.

## THE WINTER ALLOTMENT

In the chill of winter most allotment holders slow down. It is a good idea to visit at least once a fortnight to check that all is well, to prune, mend and repair while the land is fallow. There might still be produce to enjoy, including leeks, celery, cabbage, corn salad, sprouting broccoli, Chinese greens, leaf beet, Brussels sprouts, spinach and salsify, apart from the stores from summer.

Then gardeners can put their feet up by the fire, reflect on the previous year, study the plant catalogues and dream up next year's plan of action. The beauty of growing mostly annuals, which is what the majority of allotmenteers do, is that every year there is a fresh start and a blank canvas to try something new.

With gardening you go on learning forever.

▷ Even in winter, you can still go to your allotment for healthy, fresh vegetables, such as winter cabbages.

# FURTHER reading

*AGM Plants* [plants given an Award of Garden Merit]
(Royal Horticultural Society, published annually)

*The Allotment: Its Landscape and Culture*, David Crouch
and Colin Ward (Five Leaves Publications, 1997)

*Bob Flowerdew's Complete Fruit Book* (Kyle Cathie, 2000)

*Bob Flowerdew's Organic Bible* (Kyle Cathie, 1998)

*City Fields, Country Gardens: Allotment Essays*, Michael
Hyde (Five Leaves Publications, 1998)

*The Cutting Garden: Growing and Arranging Garden
Flowers*, Sarah Raven (Frances Lincoln, 1996)

*Gardener Cook*, Christopher Lloyd (Frances Lincoln,
1997)

*Gardening under Plastic*, Bernard Salt (Batsford, 1998)

*Heritage Vegetables*, Sue Stickland (Gaia Books, 1998)

*The Organic Garden Book*, Geoff Hamilton (Dorling
Kindersley, 1987)

*Organic Gardening*, Pauline Pears and Sue Stickland
(Mitchell Beazley, 1999)

*Oriental Vegetables: The Complete Guide for the
Gardening Cook*, Joy Larkcom (John Murray, 1997)

*The Permaculture Garden*, Graham Bell (Thorsons, 1994)

*Pests: How to Control them on Fruit and Vegetables*,
Pauline Pears and Bob Sherman (Henry Doubleday
Research Association/Search Press, 1992)

*RHS Pests & Diseases: The Complete Guide to
Preventing, Identifying and Treating Plant Problems*,
Pippa Greenwood and Andrew Halstead (Dorling
Kindersley, 1997).

*RHS Propagating Plants,* ed. Alan Toogood (Dorling
Kindersley, 1999)

*RHS Essential Pruning and Training*, Christopher Brickell
and David Joyce (Dorling Kindersley, 1999)

*Soil Care and Management*, Jo Readman (Henry
Doubleday Research Association/Search Press, 1991)

*Urban Gardener*, Elspeth Thompson (Orion Books, 1999)

*Vegetables*, Roger Phillips and Martyn Rix (Pan Books,
1993)

*Weeds: How to Control and Love Them*, Jo Readman
(Henry Doubleday Research Association /Search Press,
1991)

*Kitchen Garden Magazine*, Subscription Dept., Warners,
West Street, Bourne, Lincolnshire PE10 9PH.
Tel: 01778 391134

# USEFUL addresses

## ALLOTMENT ASSOCIATIONS

*These work to preserve allotments. They deal with central and local government and attend public enquiries. They offer advice to committees, individual members and the public. Many have a newsletter and provide low-cost seed in bulk to committees.*

### AUSTRIA
Zentralverband der Kleingärtner
Seidler und Kleinterzüchter
Osterreichs, Getreidemarkt 11/10
1060 Vienna
Tel: (+43) 1 587 0785
Fax: (+43) 1 587 078 x30
E-mail: zvwien@chello.at

### BELGIUM
National Verbond van Volkstuinen
Ligue National des Coins de Terre
et du Foyer – Jardins Populaire
Oudburgweg 6
9830 St Martins-Latem
Tel: (+32) 9 329 8522
Fax: (+32) 9 329 8522

### DENMARK
Kolonihaveforbundet for Denmark
Frederikssundsvej 304A
2700 Brønshøj
Tel: (+45) 382 88750
Fax: (+45) 382 88350
E-mail: info@kolonihave.dk
www.kolonihave.dk

### FINLAND
Suomen Siirtolapuutarhaliitto ry
Pengerkatu 9 B 39
00530 Helsinki
Tel: (+358) 9 763 155
Fax: (+358) 9 763 125
E-mail: sgarden@
siirtolapuutarhaliitto.fi
www.siirtolapuutarhaliitto.fi

### FRANCE
Ligue Française du Coin
de Terre et du Foyer
Fédération Nationale
des Jardins Familiaux
11 Rue Desprez
75014 Paris
Tel: (+33) 1 45 40 40 45
Fax: (+33) 1 45 40 78 90
E-mail: jardinfa@club.internet.fr

### GERMANY
Bundesverband Deutscher
Gartenfreunde e.V.
Steinerstrasse 52
53255 Bonn
Tel: (+49) 228 473 036/7
Fax: (+49) 228 476 379
E-mail: bdg@kleingarten-bund.de
www.kleingarten-bund.de

### LUXEMBOURG
Ligue Luxembourgeoise du Coin
de Terre et du Foyer
97 Rue de Bonnevoie
1260 Luxembourg
Tel: (+352) 480 199
Fax: (+352) 409 798
E-mail: liguectf@pt.lu

### THE NETHERLANDS
Algemeen Verbond van
Volkstuiners Vereningen
in Nederland
Kemphaanweg 1
1358 AA Almere
Tel: (+31) 36 538 4436
Fax: (+31) 36 538 4437

### NORWAY
Norsk Kolonihageforbund
Grondlandsleiret 23
0190 Oslo
Tel: (+47) 22 172 371
Fax: (+47) 22 173 371

### POLAND
Polski Zwiazek Dzialkowow
Krajowa Rada
ul. Grzybowsk a 4
00-131 Warsaw
Tel: (+48) 22 654 6232
Fax: (+48) 22 620 6112

### SWEDEN
Svenska Förbundet för
Koloniträdgårdar och Fritidsbyar
Åsögatan 149
11632 Stockholm
Tel: (+46) 8 743 0090
Fax: (+46) 8 640 3898
E-mail: kansli@koloni.org
www.koloni.org

### SWITZERLAND
Schweizer Familiengärtnerverband
St. Georgenstrasse 71G
9000 Sd. Gallen
Tel/Fax: (+41) 71 222 9826

## UNITED KINGDOM

The National Society of Allotment
 and Leisure Gardeners
O'Dell House
Hunters Road, Corby
Northants NN17 5JE
Tel: (+44) (0)1536 266 576
Fax: (+44) (0)1536 264 509
E-mail: natsoc@
 nsalg.demon.co.uk
www.nsalg.demon.co.uk

## UNITED STATES OF AMERICA

American Community Garden
 Association
100 N. 20th Street, 5th Floor
Philadelphia
PA 19103-1495
Tel: (+1) 215 988 8785
Fax: (+1) 215 988 8810
E-mail: smccabe@pennhort.org

National Gardening Association
1100 Dorset Street
Burlington
VT 05401
Tel: (+1) 802 863 5251
Fax: (+1) 802 864 6889
www.nationalgardening.com

San Francisco League of Urban
 Gardeners (SLUG)
2088 Oakdale Street
San Francisco
CA 94124
Tel: (+1) 415 285 SLUG
Fax: (+1) 415 285 7586

# ORGANIZATIONS

## UNITED KINGDOM

Federation of City Farms
 and Community Gardens
The Green House
Hereford Street
Bedminster
Bristol BS3 4NA.
Tel: (+44) (0)117 923 1800
Fax:(+44) (0)117 923 1900
E-mail: admin@farmgarden.org.uk
www.farmgarden.org.uk
*Provides information and advice
on a wide range of community
projects throughout the UK.*

The Henry Doubleday Research
 Association (HDRA)
Henry Doubleday Foundation
Ryton Organic Gardens
Ryton-on-Dunsmore
Coventry CV8 3LG
Tel: (+44) (0)24 7630 3517
Fax: (+44) (0)24 7663 9229
E-mail: enquiry@hdra.org.uk
www.hdra.org.uk
*HDRA is an international organiza-
tion researching and promoting
organic gardening, farming and
food. It runs a consultancy service
and a heritage Seed Library to pre-
serve threatened varieties. It also
produces a range of books as well
as the magazine,* The Organic Way.

Sustain: The Alliance for Better
 Food and Farming
94 White Lion Street
London N1 9PF
Tel: (+44) (0)20 7837 1228
Fax: (+44) (0)20 7837 1141
E-mail:sustain@sustainweb.org
www.sustainweb.org
*Works to promote a better food
policy, including projects on
growing food in cities.*

The Permaculture Association
BCM Permaculture Association
London WC1N 3XX
Tel/Fax: (+44) (0)7041 390170
E-mail: office@permaculture.org.uk
www.permaculture.org.uk
*The Permaculture Association is
an education and research charity
which supports individuals and
groups on permaculture projects.*

The Royal Horticultural Society
80 Vincent Square
London SW1P 2PE.
Tel:(+44) (0)20 7834 4333
Mail order: (+44) (0)1483 211 320
www.rhs.org.uk
*The RHS is an organization, with
show gardens at Wisley in Surrey,
Rosemoor in Devon and Hyde Hall
in East Anglia. Membership gives
you free entry to these, a monthly
copy of the magazine,* The Garden, *entry to Chelsea and Hampton
Court Palace Flower Shows and
gardening advice. The society also
offers soil testing and publishes*
AGM Plants *every year, which lists
those plants which have been
given an Award of Garden Merit.*

The Soil Association
Bristol House
40-56 Victoria Street
Bristol BS1 6BY
Tel: (+44) (0)117 929 0661
Fax: (+44) (0)117 925 2504
E-mail: info@
 soilassociation.org.uk
www.soilassociation.org.uk
*The Soil Association is an organi-
zation at the heart of the campaign
for organic food and farming.*

# SUPPLIERS AND SEED ORGANIZATIONS

## AUSTRIA

Arche Noah
Ober Strasse 40
3553 Schloss Schiltern
Tel: (+43) 2734 8626
Fax: (+43) 2734 8627
*A seed-saving network
 for members.*

## CANADA

Seeds of Diversity Canada
PO Box 36
Station Q
Toronto
Ontario M4T 2LF
*Mail-order service.*

## FINLAND

SESAM
PO Box 140
00251 Helsingore
Tel: (+358) 9 703 00721
Fax: (+358) 9 703 00791

## FRANCE

Club Mémoire Verte
BP 20
33670 La Sauve Majeure
*Mail-order service.*

Centre Régional de Ressources
 Génétiques
Ferme de Heron
Chemin de la Ferme Langlet
59650 Villenueve-d'Ascq
Tel: (+33) 20 67 0351
Fax: (+33) 20 67 0337

## IRELAND

Irish Seed Savers' Association
Capparoe, Scariff
Co Clare
Tel: (+353) 61 921 866
E-mail: issa@esatclear.ie
www.catalase.com

## SWEDEN

SESAM
Snödroppsvägen
146 50 Tullinge
Tel: (+46) 8 778 4851
Fax: (+46) 8 608 2177
E-mail: foreningen.sesam@
 telia.com

## UNITED KINGDOM

Chase Organics
The Organic Gardening Catalogue
Riverdene Business Park
Molesey road, Hesham
Surrey KT12 4RG
Tel: (+44) (0)1932 253 666
Fax: (+44) (0)1932 252707
E-mail: chaseorg@aol.com
www.organiccatalog.com
*Suppliers of organic seeds.*

H & T Proctor
Phoenix House, 51 Queen Square
Bristol BS1 4LJ
Tel: (+44) (0)117 311 1217
Fax: (+44) (0)117 311 1218
*Suppliers of organic fertilizers.*

Mayflower Gardens Ltd
Cradge Bank, Spalding
Lincolnshire. PE11 3AQ
Tel: (+44) (0)1775 766 818
Fax: (+44) (0)1775 766 919
*Suppliers of quality flower bulbs,
onion sets, peas, beans and grass
seed to allotment societies or
horticultural clubs. Catalogue
available on request.*

Peter Nyssen Ltd
124 Flixton Road
Urmston
Manchester M41 5BG
Tel: (+44) (0)161 748 6666
*Excellent bulbs sold in quantity
with a minimum order of fifty.*

Terre de Semences
Ripple Farm
Crundale, Canterbury
Kent CT4 7EB
Tel: (+44) (0)966 448379
www.terredesemences.com
*Suppliers of organic seeds.*

## USA

Seed Savers Exchange
3076 North Winn Road
Decorah, IA 52101
Tel: (+1) 319 382 5990
Fax: (+1) 319 382 587

# INDEX

## ACKNOWLEDGEMENTS

I would like to thank the many allotmenteers I have been honoured to meet in the course of writing this book. They have put up with my impositions with great good humour and have been very generous with their time. My particular thanks go to Jean Keiffer and Annie Hoffman, who gave up their weekend to drive me around allotments in Luxembourg and in and out of France and Belgium; and to Herman Vroklage who sent me on a fascinating tour of Amsterdam's leisure gardens. Perhaps the most stunning was Amstelglorie, which is run on innovative organic principles, and I thank Wim Hemker, the gardener who has made it his life's work, for showing it to me. I am eternally grateful to one of my lifelong friends, Bill Scobie, who read the text (I fear with raised eyebrows) but came up with excellent criticism, as always. The same goes for Dr Richard Wiltshire, QED Allotments, Dartford, who set me on the right track in the beginning and became my mentor at the end; also to Allan Rees, Chairman of the National Association of Allotments and Leisure Gardens, for a series of illuminating conversations. Last but not least, my sincerest thanks to Rosemary Wilkinson, Clare Johnson and Kate Latham at New Holland Publishers for being the best collaborators.